Jump Start Your Career
in Technology & IT
in about 100 Pages

Table of Contents

Let's Start !

Introduction

R Succinctly will introduce you to R, a powerful programming language for statistical work. This book will not turn you into a professional statistician. Instead, it will show you the basic practices in R for analyzing your own data. It will also help you understand some of the choices that go into statistical analysis.

A good rule of thumb in data analysis is to use the simplest tools and procedures that will allow you to reach your goals. In most situations, this means spreadsheets, bar charts, and pivot tables, among others. These are important tools and every analyst should be comfortable with them, but there is only so much that a spreadsheet can do. The need may arise for something more flexible and sophisticated. The statistical programming language R meets that need. The capabilities of the base installation of R are extraordinary. Even more, users can extend R with thousands of available packages (5,423 at the time of writing). With these packages—and their increasing growth—it sometimes feels as though R can do anything. This may be what led statistician Simon Blomberg to claim, in the spirit of Yoda: "This is R. There is no if, only how."

This book is brief by nature. I will not—and cannot—discuss all that R can do. I will, instead, discuss the most common and most helpful procedures for conventional data sets. I have two goals for this book. The first goal is to help you become comfortable with the R environment. The second goal is to inspire you to search for ways that R can answer your specific questions and data needs.

I hope you will find much that is useful here. R has been instrumental in my own work. I think your work will be the better for it, as well. Thank you for reading.

Preface

Before we begin exploring R, we need to mention a few points about the layout of this book and the appearance of R code.

How this book is structured

R Succinctly flows in a logical order that matches the common steps in analysis. First I will describe how to install R and the free R programming environment RStudio. Next, I will discuss some methods for entering and rearranging data. In the core sections of the text, we will look at methods for descriptive and inferential analysis. We will cover methods for analyzing one variable, then two variables, and then several variables. In each case, we will first examine visual methods of analysis and then look at statistical methods.

I believe that this bottom-to-top order is critical. A complex analysis cannot proceed without well-understood and well-behaved variables. If we skip these steps, then we could lose important insights. I also believe that it is important to start with charts before moving to numerical analyses. Humans are visual animals; we are able to take in and process enormous amounts of data by just looking. Statistical graphs or visualizations are the easiest way to understand complex data sets. The numbers are important, of course, but I believe that they exist to support the visuals and not the other way around. The visuals should be primary in analysis and this book reflects that primacy.

Focus on code

I will assume that you have a basic understanding of statistical principles and practices. As such, I will focus on the mechanics of using R to analyze data. This means that most of the text in this book will consist of the code to give R commands and the resulting output. I encourage you to try variations on the code and try adapting my samples to your own data. In this hands-on way, you can get the best understanding possible of the potential of R in your own work.

Code samples

This book uses a large number of code samples or scripts to show how R works. These code samples are available here. Each sample is an R script file or source file with the .R suffix. These are simple text files and will open in R, RStudio, or your preferred text editor.

Chapter 1 Getting Started with R

R is a free, open-source statistical programming language. Its utility and popularity show the same explosive growth that characterizes the increasing availability and variety of data. And while the command line interface of R can be intimidating at first to many people, the strengths of this approach, such as increased ability to share and reproduce analyses, soon become apparent. This book serves as an introduction to R for people who are intrigued by its possibilities. Chapter 1 will lay out the steps for installing R and a companion product, RStudio, for working with variables and data sets, and for discovering the power of the third-party packages that supplement R's functionality.

Installing R

R is a free download that is available for Windows, Mac, and Linux computers. Installation is a simple process.

1. Open a web browser and go to the R Project site.
2. Under "Getting Started," click "download R," which will take you to a list of dozens of servers with the downloads.
3. Click any of the servers, although it may work best to click the link http://cran.rstudio.com/ under "0-Cloud".
4. Click the download link for your operating system; the top option is often the best.
5. Open the downloaded file and follow the instructions to install the software.

You should now have a functional copy of R on your computer. If you double-click the application icon to open it, then you will see the default startup window in R. It looks something like Figure 1.

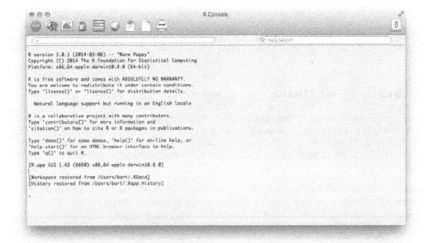

Figure 1: *The Default Startup Window for R*

For those who are comfortable working with the command line, it is also possible to access R that way. For example, if I open Terminal on my Mac and type **R** at the prompt, I get Figure 2.

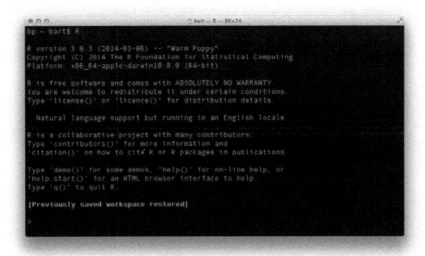

Figure 2: *Calling R from the Command Line*

You'll notice that the exact same boilerplate text that appeared in R's IDE appears in the Terminal.

Many people run R in either of these two environments: R's IDE, or the command line. 'There are other methods, though, that make working with R easier, which is where we will turn next.

Installing RStudio

R is a great way to work with data but the interface is not perfect. Part of the problem is that everything opens in separate windows. Another problem is that the default interface for R does not look and act the same in each operating system. Several interfaces for R exist to solve these problems. Although there are many choices, the interface that we will use in this book is RStudio.

Like R, RStudio is a free download that is available for Windows, Mac, and Linux computers. Again, installation is a simple process, but note that you must first install R.

1. Open a web browser and go to https://www.rstudio.com.
2. Click "Download now".
3. RStudio can run on a desktop or over a Linux server. We will use the desktop version, so click "Download RStudio Desktop."
4. RStudio will check your operating system; click the link under "Recommended for your system."
5. Open the downloaded file and follow the instructions to install the software.

If you double-click the RStudio icon, you will see something like Figure 3.

RStudio organizes the separate windows of R into a single panel. It also provides links to functions that can otherwise be difficult to find. RStudio has a few other advantages as well:

- It allows you to divide your work into contexts or "projects." Each project has its own working directory, workspace, history, and source documents.
- It has GitHub integration.
- It saves a graphics history.
- It exports graphics in many sizes and formats.
- It can create interactive graphics via the Manipulate package.
- It provides code completion with the tab key.
- It has standardized keyboard shortcuts.

RStudio is a convenient way of working with R, but there are other options. You may want to spend a little time looking at some of the alternatives so you can find what works best for you and your projects.

The R console

When you open RStudio, the two windows where you will work the most are on the left by default. The bottom window on the left is the R console, which has the R command prompt: > (the "greater than" sign). Two things can happen in the console. First, you can run commands here by typing at the prompt, although you cannot save your work there. Second, R gives the output for the commands.

We can try entering a basic command in the console to see how it works. We'll start with addition. Enter the following text at the command prompt and press Enter:

```
> 9 + 11
```

The first line contains the command you entered; in this case 9 + 11. Note that you do not need to type an equal sign or any other command terminator, such as a semicolon. Also, although it is not necessary to put spaces before and after the plus sign, it is good form.[1] The output looks like this:

```
[1] 20
```

The second line does not have a command prompt because it has the program's output. The "1" in square brackets, [1], requires some explanation. R uses vectors to do math and that it how it returns the responses. The number in brackets is the index number for the first item in the vector on this line of output. (Many other programs begin with an index number of 0, but R begins at 1.) After the index number, R prints the output, the sum "20" in this case.

---

[1] For more information on good form in R, see Google's style guide at http://google-styleguide.googlecode.com/svn/trunk/Rguide.xml.

The contents of the console will scroll up as new information comes in. You can also clear the console by selecting Edit > Clear console or pressing ctrl-l (a lower-case L) on a Mac or PC. Note that this only clears the displayed data, it does not purge the data from the memory or lose the history of commands.

The Script window

The console is the default window in R, but it is not the best place to do your work. The major problem is that you cannot save your commands. Another problem is that you can enter only one command at a time. Given these problems, a much better way to work with R is to use the Script window. In RStudio, this is the window on the top left, above the console. (In case you see nothing there, go to File > New File > R Script or press Shift+Command+N to create a new script document.)

A script in R is a plain text file with the extension ".R." When you create a new script in R, you can save that script and you can select and run one or more lines of it at a time. We can recreate the simple addition problem we did in the console by creating a new script and then typing the command again. You can also enter more than one command in a script, even if you only run one at a time. To see how this works, you should type the following three lines.

```
9 + 11
1:50
print("Hello World")
```

Note that there is no command prompt > in the script window. Instead, there are just numbered lines of text. Next, save this script by either selecting File > Save or by pressing Command+S on the Mac and Ctrl+S on Windows.

If you want to run one command at a time, then place your cursor anywhere on the line of desired command. Then select Code > Run Line(s) or press Command+Return (Ctrl+Return on Windows). This will send the selected command down to the console and display the results. For the first command, 9 + 11, this will produce the same results that we had earlier when we entered the command at the console.

The next two lines of code illustrate a few other, basic functions. The command 1:50 creates a list of numbers from 1 to 50. You can also see that the number in square brackets at the beginning of the line is the index number for the first item on that line.

```
[1]   1  2  3  4  5  6  7  8  9 10 11 12 13 14 15 16 17 18 19 20 21 22 23
[24] 24 25 26 27 28 29 30 31 32 33 34 35 36 37 38 39 40 41 42 43 44 45 46
[47] 47 48 49 50
```

If you run the third line of text, print("Hello World!"), you get this output.

```
[1] "Hello World!"
```

The output **"Hello World!"** is a character vector of length 1. This is the same as a string in C or other languages.

Comments

It is good form to add comments to your code. Comments can help you remember what each section of your code does. Comments also help make your code reproducible because other people can follow your logic. This is critical in collaborative projects, as well as projects that you might revisit later.

To make a comment in R, type # followed by your text. You can also "comment out" a line of code to disable it while you try alternative lines. To make a multiline comment, you will need to comment each line, as R has no built-in multiline function. RStudio makes it easy to comment out lines. Just select the text and go to Code > Comment/Uncomment Lines or press Shift+Command+C (Shift+Ctrl+C on Windows).

```
# These lines demonstrate commenting in R.
# First, add an inline comment on a line of code to explain it.
print("Hello World!")  # Prints "Hello World" in the console.
# Second, comment out a variation on a line of code.
# print("Hello R!")  # This line will not run while commented out.
```

Data structures

R recognizes four basic structures of data:

1. **Vectors**. A vector is a one-dimensional array. All of the data must be in the same format, such as numeric, character, and so on. This is the basic data object in R.
2. **Matrices and Arrays**. A matrix is similar to a vector in that all of the data must be of the same format. A matrix, however, has two dimensions; the data is arranged in rows and columns (and the columns must be the same length), but the columns are not named. An array is similar to a matrix except that it can have more than two dimensions.
3. **Data frames**. A data frame is a collection of vectors that are all the same length. The difference between a data frame and a matrix is that a data frame can have vectors of different data types, such as a numeric vector and a character vector. The vectors can also have names. A data frame is similar to a data sheet in SPSS or a worksheet in Excel (with the difference, again, that the vectors in a data frame must all be the same length).
4. **Lists**. A list is the most general data structure in R. A list is an ordered collection of elements of any class, length, or structure (including other lists). Many statistical functions, however, cannot be applied to lists.

R also has several built-in functions for converting or coercing data from one structure to another:

- `as.vector()` can coerce matrices to one-dimensional vectors, although it may be necessary to first coerce them to matrices
- `as.matrix()` can coerce data structures into the matrix structure
- `as.data.frame()` can coerce data structure into data frames
- `as.list()` can coerce data structures to lists

Variables

Variables are easy to create in R. Just type the name of the variable, there is no need to assign the variable type. Next, use the assignment operator, which is `<-`. You can read this as "gets," so that `x <- 2` means "x gets 2." It is possible to use the equal sign for assigning values, but that is bad form in R. In the following two lines, I create a variable x, assign the values 1 to 5, and then display the contents of x by typing its name.

```
x <- 1:5  # Put the numbers 1-5 in the variable x
x  # Displays the values in x
```

If you want to specify each value that you assign to a variable, you can use the function **c**. This stands for "concatenate," although you can also think of it as "combine" or "collection." This function will create a single vector with the items you assign to it. As a note, RStudio has a convenient shortcut for the assignment operator, `<-`. When you are typing in your code, use the shortcut Alt+Hyphen and RStudio will insert a leading space, the assignment operator, and a trailing space. You can then continue with your coding.

Here I assign the values 7, 12, 5, 4, and 9 to the vector y.

```
y <- c(7, 12, 5, 4, 9)
```

The assignment operator can also go from left to right or it can include several variables at once.

```
15 -> a  # Can go left to right, but is confusing.
a <- b <- c <- 30  # Assign the same value to multiple variables.
```

To remove a variable from R's workspace, use the **rm** function.

```
rm(x)  # Remove the object x from the workspace.
rm(a, b)  # Remove more than one object.
rm(list = ls())  # Clear the entire workspace.
```

Packages

The default installation of R is impressive in its functionality but it can't do everything. One of the great strengths of R is that you can add packages. Packages are bundles of code that extend R's capabilities. In other languages, these bundles are libraries, but in R the library is the place that stores all the packages. Packages for R can come from two different places.

Some packages ship with R but are not active by default. You can see these in the Packages tab in RStudio. Other packages are available online at repositories. A list of available packages can be viewed here. This webpage is part of the Comprehensive R Archive Network (CRAN). It contains a list of topics or "task views" for packages. If you click on a topic, it will take you to an annotated list with links to individual packages. You can also search for packages by name here. Another good option is the website CRANtastic. All the packages at these sites are, like R, free and open source.

To see which packages are currently installed or loaded, use the following functions:

```
library()  # Brings up editor list of installed packages.

search()   # Shows packages that are currently loaded.
```

`library()` will bring up a text list of functions. The same information is available in hyperlinked format under the Packages tab in RStudio. `search()` will display the names of the active packages in the console. These are the same packages that have checks in RStudio's Package tab.

To install new packages, you have several options in RStudio. First, you can use the menus under Tools > Install Packages. Second, you can click "Install Packages" at the top of the Packages tab. Third, you can use the function `install.packages()`. Just put the name of the desired package in quotes (and remember that, like most programming languages, R is case-sensitive). The last option is best if you want to save the command as part of a script.

```
install.packages("ggplot2")  # Download and install the ggplot2 package.
```

The previous command installs the package. To use the package, you must also load it or make it active in R. There are two ways to do this. The first is `library()`, which is often used for loading packages in scripts. The second is `require()`, which is often used for loading packages in functions.[2] In my experience, `require()`, works in either setting and avoids confusion about the meaning of "library," so I prefer to use it.

```
library("ggplot2")  # Makes package available; often used in scripts.

require("ggplot2")  # Also makes package available; often used in functions.
```

---

[2] In the current version of R—I am using version 3.0.3 as I write this—it is not always necessary to put quotes around the package name. I would still recommend that you use quotes around the package names for two reasons: (1) it increases cross-version compatibility, and (2) this is how the code appears in the console if you check the package by hand in RStudio's package list.

To learn more about a package, you can use R's built-in help functions. Many packages also have vignettes, which are examples of the package's functions. You can access these with the following code:

```
vignette(package = "grid")  # Brings up list of vignettes in editor window
?vignette  # For help on vignettes in general
browseVignettes(package = "grid")  # Open webpage with hyperlinks
vignette()  # List of all vignettes for currently installed packages
browseVignettes()  # HTML for all vignettes for currently installed packages
```

You should also check for package updates on a regular basis. There are three ways to do this. First, you can use the menus in RStudio: Tools > Check for Package Updates. Second, you can go the Package tab in RStudio and click "Check for Updates." Third, you can run this command: `update.packages()`.

When you finish working in R, you may want to unload or remove packages that you won't use again soon. By default, R unloads all packages when it quits. If you want to unload them before then, you have two options. First, you can go to the Packages tab in RStudio and uncheck the packages one by one. Second, you can use the `detach()` command, like this: `detach("package:ggplot2", unload = TRUE)`.[3]

If you would like to delete a package, use `remove.packages()`, like this: `remove.packages("psytabs")`. This trashes the packages. If you want to use a deleted package again you will need to download it and reinstall it.

R's datasets package

The built-in package "datasets" makes it easy to experiment with R's procedures using real data. Although this package is part of R's base installation, you must load it. You can either select it in the Packages tab or enter `library("datasets")` or `require("datasets")`. You can see a list of the available data sets by typing `data()` or by going to the R Datasets Package list.

---

[3] It is possible to run `detach()` without quotes around the package name, like this: `detach(package:ggplot2)`. It is also possible to run the command without specifying "`unload = TRUE`," but you could have problems with uncleared namespaces. The reason I suggest `detach("package:ggplot2", unload = TRUE)` is because that is how R shows the code when you uncheck the package by hand. This is the method that is least prone to errors. Also, if you receive an invalid 'name' argument error, then add `character.only = TRUE` to the command.

For more information on a particular data set, you can search R help by typing **?** and the name of the data set with no space: **?airmiles**. You can also see the contents of the data set by entering its name: **airmiles**. To see the structure of the data set, use **str()**, like this: **str(airmiles)**. That will show you what kind of data set it is, how many observations and variables it has, and the first few values.

If you are ready to work with the data set, you can load it with **data()**, like this: **data(airmiles)**. It will then appear in the Environment tab in the top right of RStudio.

R's built-in data sets are a wonderful resource. You can use them to try out different functions and procedures without having to find or enter data. We'll use these data sets in every chapter of this book. I suggest that you take a little while to look through them to see what may be of interest to you.

Entering data manually

R is flexible in that it allows you to get data into the program in many different ways.

The simplest—but not always the fastest—is to enter the data right into R. If you only have a handful of values, then this method might make sense.

If you want to create patterned data, you have two common choices. First, the colon operator **:** creates a set of sequential integer values. For example:

```
0:10
```

Gives this ascending list:

```
[1]  0  1  2  3  4  5  6  7  8  9 10
```

Or, by placing the larger number first, as shown here:

```
55:48
```

Then R will create a descending list:

```
[1] 55 54 53 52 51 50 49 48
```

Another choice for patterned data is the sequence function **seq()**, which is more flexible.

You can choose the step size:

```
seq(30, 0, by = -3)
```

This size yields the following:

```
[1] 30 27 24 21 18 15 12  9  6  3  0
```

Or you can choose the list length:

```
seq(0, 5, length.out = 11)
```

Which gives you:

```
[1] 0.0 0.5 1.0 1.5 2.0 2.5 3.0 3.5 4.0 4.5 5.0
```

You can also feed any of these functions into a new variable. Just declare the variable name and put the assignment operator before the function, like this:

```
x <- seq(50, 150, by = 5)
```

If, instead, you have real data that are not sequenced, you can enter them into R two ways. First, you can use the concatenate function c() as mentioned earlier. For example:

```
x <- c(5, 4, 1, 6, 7, 2, 2, 3, 2, 8)
```

Second, you can enter the numbers in the console using the scan() function. After calling this function, go to the console and type one number at a time. Press return after each number. When you finish, press return twice to send the data to the variable.

In my experience, it only makes sense to enter data into R if you have sequential data or toy data. For a data set of any real size, it is almost always easier to import the data into R, which is what we will discuss next.

Importing data

An enormous amount of data resides in spreadsheets. R makes it easy to import such data, with some important qualifications. Many people also have data in statistical programs such as SPSS or SAS. R is also able to read that data, but again with an important qualification.

Avoid native files from Excel or SPSS

Don't try to import native Excel spreadsheets or SPSS files. While there are packages designed to do both of these, they are often difficult to use and they can introduce problems. The R website[4] says this about importing Excel spreadsheets (emphasis added):

> The most common R data import/export question seems to be "how do I read an Excel spreadsheet" ... The first piece of advice is to **avoid doing so if possible!** If you have access to Excel, export the data you want from Excel in tab-delimited or comma-separated form, and use **read.delim** or **read.csv** to import it into R ... [An] Excel .xls file is not just a spreadsheet: such files can contain many sheets, and the sheets can contain formulae, macros and so on. Not all readers can read other than the first sheet, and may be confused by other contents of the file.

Many of the same problems apply to SPSS files. The good news is that there is a simple solution to these problems.

Importing CSV files

The easiest way to import data into R is with a CSV file, or comma-separated values spreadsheet. Any spreadsheet program, including Excel, can save files in the CSV format. Statistical programs like SPSS can do this, too.[5] Then, to read a CSV file, use the **read.csv** function. You will need to specify the location of the file and whether it has a header row for variable names. For example, on my Mac, I could import a file named "rawdata.csv" from my desktop this way:

```
csvdata <- read.csv("~/Desktop/rawdata.csv", header = TRUE)
```

A similar process can read data in tab-delimited TXT files. The differences are these: First, use **read.table** instead of **read.csv**. Second, you may need to be explicit about the separator, such as a comma or a tab, by specifying that in the command. Third, if you have missing data values, be sure to specify an unambiguous separator for the cells. If your separators are tabs, then use the command **sep = \t**, as in this example:

```
txtdata <- read.table("~/Desktop/rawdata.txt", header = TRUE, sep = "\t")
```

R and its available packages offer a variety of ways to get data into the program. I have found, though, that it is almost always easiest to put the data into a CSV file and import that. But regardless of how you get your data into R, now you are ready to begin exploring your data.

---

[4] See http://cran.r-project.org/doc/manuals/R-data.html#Reading-Excel-spreadsheets
[5] To save an SPSS SAV file as a CSV file, use these two options in the "Save As" dialog: (a) "Write variable names to spreadsheet"; and (b) "Save value labels where defined instead of data values."

Converting tabular data to row data

One important question to ask right away is whether your data are in the right format for your analyses. This is most important for categorical data, because it is possible to collapse the data into frequency counts. An excellent example is the built-in R data set `UCBAdmissions`. This data set describes outcomes for graduate admissions at UC Berkeley in 1973. These data are important because they formed the basis of a major discrimination lawsuit. They are also a perfect example of Simpson's Paradox[6] in statistics. Before we take a look at the code, I should explain two things.

First, tabular data are data that can be organized into tables with rows and columns of frequencies. For example, you could create a table that showed the popularity of several Internet browsers. That table would have just one dimension or factor: which browser was installed. You could then add a second dimension that broke down the data by operating system. The browsers would be listed in the columns and the operating systems would be listed in the rows. This would be a two-way table, or cross-tabulation. The numbers in each cell of the table would give you the number of cases that matched that combination of categories, such as the number of Windows PCs running IE or the number of Android tablets running Chrome. It is, of course, possible to add more variables, which would usually be shown as separate panels or tables, each of which would have the same rows and columns. This is also the case in the UCBAdmissions data that we'll use in this example. The data are arranged in rows and columns (or panels) to get "marginal" totals, which are more often just called "marginals." These marginals are the totals for one or more variables summed across other variables. So, for example, in our hypothetical table of browsers and operating systems, the marginal for browsers would be the total number of installations of each browser, ignoring the operating systems. In a similar manner, the marginals for the operating system would give the total number of installations for each OS, ignoring the browser. The marginals are important because they are often of greater interest than the data at maximum dimensionality (i.e., where all of the dimensions or factors are broken down to their most detailed level).

Second, I am going to use two plotting commands in this example—barplot() and plot()—and the next on color that I have not yet presented. Right now I am using them to demonstrate other principles but I will explain them fully in the next chapter on graphics.

The code for this section is available in a single R file, sample_1_1.R, but I will break it into parts for readability.

Sample: sample_1_1.R

```
# LOAD DATA
require("datasets")  # Load datasets package
?UCBAdmissions  # Data from graduate admissions at UC Berkeley in 1973.
str(UCBAdmissions)  # Tabular data in 3 dimensions; N = 4526.
```

---

[6] See http://vudlab.com/simpsons/, which has insightful commentary and interactive graphics for this data set.

```
UCBAdmissions   # Prints six tables; one for each department.

# TRY DEFAULT PLOTS
admit.fail <- (UCBAdmissions$Admit)   # Doesn't work.
barplot(UCBAdmissions$Admit)   # Doesn't work.
plot(UCBAdmissions)   # Makes a plot, but not the one we wanted.
```

This code produces Figure 4, which is an unusual 3-way bar plot. We wanted a simple bar chart of the number of people who applied to each of the six departments, so this doesn't work.

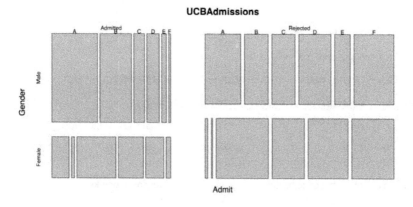

Figure 4:   *Default Plot of UCBAdmissions*

The next step is to get the marginal frequencies from the 3-way table. At this point, the frequencies are just displayed in the console.

```
# SHOW MARGINAL FREQUENCIES
margin.table(UCBAdmissions, 1)   # Admit
margin.table(UCBAdmissions, 2)   # Gender
margin.table(UCBAdmissions, 3)   # Dept
margin.table(UCBAdmissions)      # Total
```

Next we save the marginal frequency for department, as this has the data we need for the chart.

```
# SAVE MARGINALS
admit.dept <- margin.table(UCBAdmissions, 3)   # Creates table for dept
```

```
str(admit.dept)  # Describe the structure of the data table
barplot(admit.dept)  # Makes a default barplot of the frequencies
admit.dept  # Show frequencies
prop.table(admit.dept)  # Show as proportions
round(prop.table(admit.dept), 2)  # Show as proportions w/2 digits
round(prop.table(admit.dept), 2) * 100  # Percentages w/o decimals
```

However, further analyses need the data to be structured as one row per person. We can do that by converting from a table to a data frame to a list to a data frame.

```
# RESTRUCTURE DATA

admit1 <- as.data.frame.table(UCBAdmissions)  # Coerces to data frame

# This repeats each row by Freq

admit2 <- lapply(admit1, function(x)rep(x, admit1$Freq))

admit3 <- as.data.frame(admit2)  # Converts from list back to data frame.

admit4 <- admit3[, -4]  # Removes fifth column that has frequencies.

# admit4 is the final data set, ready for analysis by case.
```

It is also possible, though substitution, to do the entire conversion in one long command:

```
# COMBINE ALL STEPS
admit.rows <- as.data.frame(lapply(as.data.frame.table(UCBAdmissions),
function(x)rep(x, as.data.frame.table(UCBAdmissions)$Freq)))[, -4]
```

The commands above show one way to organize data into the structure that will be most useful for analysis. In other situations different approaches will be more helpful, but this gives you a useful idea of what you can do in R.

Color

When you make graphs in R, you should consider your design decisions. Factors like layout and color can make or break visualizations. Consider a bar chart made with R's default colors.

Sample: sample_1_2.R

```
# LOAD DATA
x = c(12, 4, 21, 17, 13, 9)  # Data for bar chart
```

The following command uses the default colors.

```
# BARPLOT WITH DEFAULT COLORS
barplot(x)  # Default barplot
```

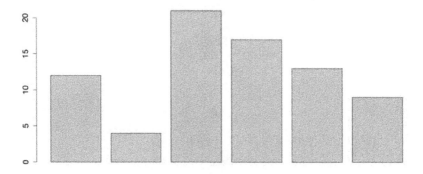

Figure 5:   *Bar Chart with Default Colors*

We could improve Figure 5 by changing the colors of the bars using the **col** attribute in the **barplot** function. R gives us several methods to specify colors.

R has names for 657 colors, arranged in alphabetical order (except for white, which is first on the list). You can see a text list of all the color names by entering **colors()**. You can also see a PDF with color charts here. If I want to change the bars to slategray3, I can do this in several ways:

- Color name: slategray3.
- Color location in list: slategray3 is index number 602 in the vector of colors.
- RGB hex codes: According to this Stowers Institute chart, slategray3 is #9FB6CD
- RGB color on a 0-255 scale: Use **col2rgb("slategray3")** to get 159, 182, and 205 or see the values on the previous PDF. You must specify 255 as the maximum value.
- RGB color on a 0-1 scale: Divide the previous values by 255 to get .62, .71, and .80.

You can then use these values in the **col** attribute:

```
# METHODS TO SPECIFY COLORS
```

```
barplot(x, col = "slategray3")  # Color by name.
barplot(x, col = colors() [602])  # slategray3 is 602 in the list.
barplot(x, col = "#9FB6CD ")  # RGB hex code.
barplot(x, col = rgb(159, 182, 205, max = 255))  # RGB 0-255
barplot(x, col = rgb(.62, .71, .80))  # RGB 0.00-1.00
```

Any of the previous commands will produce the chart in Figure 6.

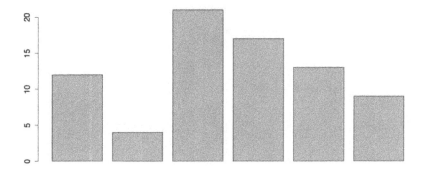

Figure 6:   *Colored Bar Chart*

If you want to the bars to be different colors, then you can either specify the colors one at a time or you can use a color palette. To specify the individual colors, just use the concatenate function **c()** in the **col** attribute, like this: **col = c("red", "blue")**. You can use any of the color specification methods in the section. The colors will then cycle through for each of the bars.

A palette can give a wider range of colors, as well as colors that look better together. You can use R's built-in palettes by specifying the name of the palette and the number of colors you desire. Some of R's palettes are:

- rainbow: bright primary colors
- heat.colors: yellow through red
- terrain.colors: gray through green
- topo.colors: purple through tan
- cm.colors: blues and pinks

Run the command **?palette** for more information on R's built-in palettes.

To use the topo.colors palette for the six bars, you would enter the following:

```
# BARPLOT WITH BUILT-IN PALETTE
barplot(x, col = topo.colors(6))
```

The output of the previous code is shown in Figure 7.

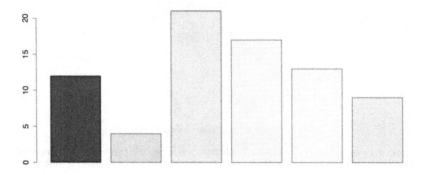

Figure 7:   *Bar Chart with the R Palette "topo.colors"*

An attractive alternative to R's palettes is the package RColorBrewer. This package derives from the excellent website ColorBrewer 2.0.[7] RColorBrewer provides several palettes of sequential, diverging, and qualitative colors. To use RColorBrewer, you must first install it and load it in R:

```
# INSTALL AND LOAD RCOLORBREWER PACKAGE
install.packages("RColorBrewer")
require("RColorBrewer")
```

I encourage you to explore the help information for RColorBrewer by entering **help(package = "RColorBrewer")**. You can see all the available palettes by entering **display.brewer.all()**. This produces Figure 8. (The overlapping labels are due to the landscape aspect ratio.)

---

[7] Another great resource for color palettes is Adobe's Kuler website at https://kuler.adobe.com.

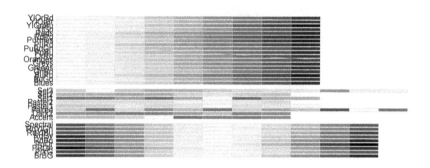

Figure 8: *All RColorBrewer Palettes*

You can get a better view of an individual palette by specifying the palette and the number of colors desired, like this: `display.brewer.pal(8, "Accent")`. Figure 9 illustrates this palette.

Accent (qualitative)

Figure 9: *Preview of the RColorBrewer Palette "Accent"*

To apply an RColorBrewer palette to a bar chart, call `brewer.pal` in the `col` attribute. Also specify the palette and the number of colors desired.

```
# BARPLOT WITH RCOLORBREWER PALETTE
```

```
barplot(x, col = brewer.pal(6, "Blues"))
```

This command produces Figure 10.

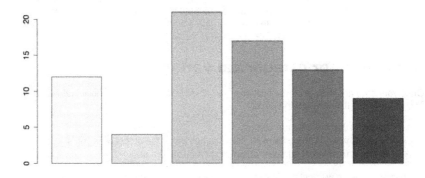

Figure 10: *Bar Chart with RColorBrewer Palette*

When you finish, it is a good idea to restore the default palette and clean up:

```
# CLEAN UP
palette("default")  # Return to default palette.
detach("package:RColorBrewer", unload = TRUE)  # Unloads RColorBrewer
rm(list = ls())  # Removes all objects from workspace.
```

Chapter 2 Charts for One Variable

In the Preface I mentioned that analyses are most useful when graphics come first, before the statistical procedures. In addition, the individual variables that form the basis of all later work need to be well understood and, if appropriate, adapted to the analytical needs. With those two points in mind, Chapter 2 begins with charts for one variable.

Bar charts for categorical variables

Once your data are in R, your first task in any analysis is to examine the individual variables. The purposes of this task are threefold:

- To check that the data are correct.
- To check whether the data meet the assumptions of the procedures you will use.
- To check for interesting observations or patterns in the data.

It is easiest to begin with categorical variables, such as a respondent's gender or a company's sector. Bar charts work well for such data, so that is where we turn first.

For this example, we will use **chickwts** from R's **datasets** package. This data set records the weights of chicks and the feed that they had. To see more on this data set, enter **?chickwts**. To see the entire data set in the console—it has 71 cases—enter **chickwts**. To make the plot, we need to run the following two commands:

Sample: sample_2_1.R

```
# LOAD DATA
require("datasets")   # Loads data sets package
```

Then run the default **plot()** command.

```
# DEFAULT CHART WITH PLOT()
plot(chickwts$feed)   # Default method to plot the variable feed from chickwts
```

The default **plot()** function is adaptive. It will produce different charts depending on what variable(s) you give it. If you give it a categorical variable, as we have done here, it produces the bar chart in Figure 11. The argument, **chickwts$feed**, is a way of telling R to use the data set "chickwts" and then the variable "feed" from that data set.

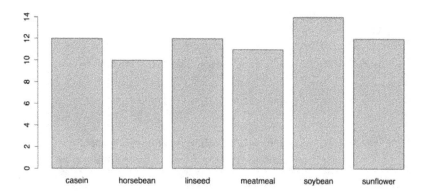

Figure 11: *A Default Bar Chart from the* plot() *Function*

The chart in Figure 11 is functional but it lacking in several respects. We should add titles, rearrange the bars, and change the margins, among other things. The default **plot()** function, though, does not provide much control. Instead, we will need to use the **barplot()** function. But first, we will need to calculate the frequencies for the chart. We can use the **table()** function for that:

```
# CREATE TABLE
feeds <- table(chickwts$feed)  # Create a table of feed, place in "feeds"
feeds  # See contents of object "feeds"
barplot(feeds)  # Identical to plot(chickwts$feed) but with new object
```

Now we can create a new chart using **barplot()**. We will also adjust a few parameters with the **par()** function. (Enter **?par** for more information.) R gives you two choices for running multiline commands from the Script window. You can run one line at a time by pressing Command+Return (Ctrl+Return on Windows) for each line. In this case, nothing will happen until you run the last line of the command. You can also highlight the block and run it at once with the same keyboard command.

```
# USE BARPLOT() AND PAR() FOR PARAMETERS
par(oma = c(1, 4, 1, 1))  # Sets outside margins: bottom, left, top, right.
par(mar = c(4, 5, 2, 1))  # Sets plot margins.
barplot(feeds[order(feeds)],  # Orders the bars by descending values.
        horiz = TRUE,  # Makes the bars horizontal.
        las   = 1,  # las gives orientation of axis labels.
```

```
col     = c("beige", "blanchedalmond", "bisque1", "bisque2",
            "bisque3", "bisque4"),  # Vector of colors for bars.
border = NA,  # No borders on bars.
# Add main title and label for x-axis.
main    = "Frequencies of Different Feeds in chickwts Data set",
xlab    = "Number of Chicks")
```

This series of commands will produce the modified bar chart in Figure 12.

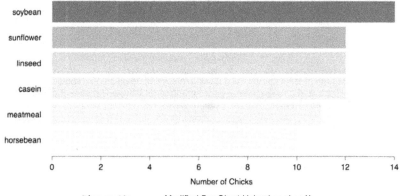

Figure 12:   *Modified Bar Chart Using barplot()*

Finish by saving your work, resetting the graphics parameters, and clearing the workspace of unneeded variables, objects, and packages:

```
# CLEAN UP
par(oldpar)  # Restores previous parameters (ignore errors).
detach("package:datasets", unload = TRUE)  # Unloads data sets package.
rm(list = ls())  # Removes all objects from workspace.
```

Saving charts in R and RStudio

There are two ways to save charts so you can export them. The first method, which is the default method for R, is cumbersome and confusing but you can include it in your code. The second method, which uses RStudio, is much simpler but uses menus. (I have used the second method for all the images in this book.)

To save images using R's method, you must open a device or "graphical device." The following code shows how to use devices to save either PNG files for raster graphics or PDF files for vector graphics. (You must use one or the other for the command; you cannot run both at once. There are also several other formats available.) See **?png**, **?pdf**, and **?dev** for more information on these functions.

Sample: sample_2_2.R

```
# CHOOSE GRAPHICS DEVICE
# TO SAVE AS PNG
# EITHER this device for a PNG file (raster graphics)
png(filename = "~/Desktop/bar_a.png",  # Give the full path and name.
    width = 900,  # Width of image in pixels.
    height = 600)  # Height of image in pixels.


# TO SAVE AS PDF
# OR this device for a PDF file (scalable vector graphics)
pdf("bar_b.pdf",  # Save to default directory or errors ensue.
    width = 9,  # Width in inches (NOT pixels).
    height = 6)  #Height in inches.
```

After you have selected a graphics device and set the parameters, then you create the graphic.

```
# CREATE GRAPHIC
# Then run the command(s) for the graphic.
oldpar <- par()  # Stores current graphical parameters.
par(oma = c(1, 1, 1, 1))  # Sets outside margins: bottom, left, top, right.
par(mar = c(4, 5, 2, 1))  # Sets plot margins.
barplot(feeds[order(feeds)],  # Order the bars by descending values.
        horiz = TRUE,  # Make the bars horizontal.
        las   = 1,  # las gives orientation of axis labels.
        col   = c("beige", "blanchedalmond", "bisque1", "bisque2",
```

```
                    "bisque3", "bisque4"),  # Vector of colors for bars
        border = NA,  # No borders on bars.
        # Add main title and label for x-axis.
        main   = "Frequencies of Different Feeds\nin chickwts Data set",
        xlab   = "Number of Chicks")
```

Once you have saved your work, you should clean the workspace of unneeded variables and objects. It is critical to turn off the graphics device with **dev.off()**.

```
# CLEAN UP
dev.off()  # Turns off graphics device.
par(oldpar)  # Restores previous graphics parameters (ignore errors).
rm(list = ls())  # Removes all objects from workspace.
```

The graph is then saved without being displayed in RStudio. As a note, you will receive several error messages when you restore the previous graphical parameters with **par(oldpar)**. These errors happen because a few of the parameters that were stored are read-only. These parameters were not modified so you can safely ignore these error messages.

I have found this method with graphical devices to be unreliable. For example, with the PNG device you must specify the full file path and save the image where you want it. But with the PDF device, the file won't open if you specify the path. Instead, you need to save the PDF to the default directory and then move it. Also, the devices do not always turn off as expected. When that happens, RStudio will not show new graphics in the Plots tab. You may need to restart RStudio to quit the devices completely. This is unnecessary frustration.

With this in mind, I prefer to use the second method for saving graphics, which uses RStudio's menus. All that you need to do is create the graphic as normal and RStudio will display it in the Plots tab. Then click the Export button at the top of the window. RStudio will first ask you whether you want to save the plot as an image, as a PDF, or save it to the clipboard. It is a simple matter then to set the parameters in the window that opens. That way, you can choose the file type, the image size, and the location, among other attributes.

Pie charts

A common way to display categorical variables is with pie charts. These are easy to make in R:

Sample: sample_2_3.R

```
# LOAD DATA SET & CREATE TABLE
require("datasets")  # Loads data sets package.
```

```
feeds <- table(chickwts$feed)  # Create a table of feed, place in "feeds"
feeds  # See contents of object "feeds".

# PIE CHART WITH DEFAULTS
 pie(feeds)
```

Figure 13 shows the resulting chart.

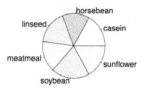

Figure 13: *Default Pie Chart*

As with bar charts, it can be helpful to modify this pie chart in a few ways:

```
# PIE CHART WITH OPTIONS
pie(feeds[order(feeds, decreasing = TRUE)],  # Order slices by values.
    init.angle = 90,  # Start as 12 o'clock instead of 3 o'clock.
    clockwise = TRUE,  # Go clockwise (default is FALSE).
    col = c("seashell", "cadetblue2", "lightpink",
            "lightcyan", "plum1", "papayawhip"),  # Change colors)
    main = "Pie Chart of Feeds from chickwts")  # Add title.
```

This produces the improved pie chart in Figure 14:

Pie Chart of Feeds from chickwts

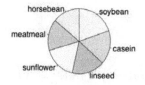

Figure 14: *Modified Pie Chart*

It is easy to make pie charts in R but it can be hard to read them. For example, the R help on pie charts (see **?pie**) says this:

Pie charts are a very bad way of displaying information. The eye is good at judging linear measures and bad at judging relative areas. A bar chart or dot chart is a preferable way of displaying this type of data.

Cleveland (1985), page 264: "Data that can be shown by pie charts always can be shown by a dot chart. This means that judgments of position along a common scale can be made instead of the less accurate angle judgments." This statement is based on the empirical investigations of Cleveland and McGill as well as investigations by perceptual psychologists.

Pie charts can be very hard to read accurately, which defeats the purpose of a graph. It is difficult to read angles and the areas of circular sectors. Comparing heights or lengths of straight bars, though, is a very simple task. For this reason, it is a good idea to avoid pie charts whenever possible and instead choose a graphic that is easier to read and interpret.

Once you have saved your work, you should clean the workspace of unneeded variables and objects:

```
# CLEAN UP
detach("package:datasets", unload = TRUE)  # Unloads data sets package
rm(list = ls())  # Removes all objects from workspace
```

Histograms

When you have a quantitative variable—that is, an interval or ratio level variable—a histogram is useful. Interval and ratio level variables both have measurable distances between scores, whereas the lower levels of measurement—nominal and ordinal—do not. For example, temperature in Fahrenheit is an interval level of measurement because it is possible to say that the high temperature for today is 2.7 degrees higher than yesterday. On the other hand, if we use an ordinal level of measurement and just say that today is hotter than yesterday, giving it a relative position but not an absolute one, then we don't know how much difference there is between the two days. In order to make a histogram, we need to know how far apart our measurements are. Interval level variables like temperature in Fahrenheit or ratio level variables that have true zero points, like distance in meters, can both do that.[8] In this example, we will use the built-in data set "lynx" (see **?lynx** for more information). First we need to load the **data sets** package and then load the **lynx** data set.

Sample: sample_2_4.R

```
# LOAD DATA SET
require("datasets")
data(lynx)  # Annual Canadian Lynx trappings 1821-1934
```

---

[8] See http://en.wikipedia.org/wiki/Level_of_measurement for more information.

`lynx` is a time series data set with only one variable, so we can just call the data set in the `hist()` function.

```
# HISTOGRAM WITH DEFAULTS
  hist(lynx)
```

This produces Figure 15:

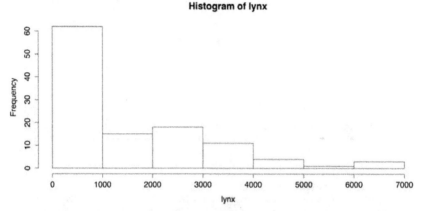

Figure 15: *Default Histogram*

Figure 15 is a respectable chart, using nothing more than the default settings. The chart has a title, the axes have labels, the number and width of bars is reasonable, and even the plain black and white is clean and easy to read. R's `hist()` function, though, has many options. Here are a few of them:

```
# HISTOGRAM WITH OPTIONS
hist(lynx,
    breaks = 14,  # "Suggests" 14 bins.
    freq = FALSE,  # Axis shows density, not frequency.
    col = "thistle1",  # Color for the histogram.
    main = "Histogram of Annual Canadian Lynx Trappings\n1821-1934",
    xlab = "Number of Lynx Trapped")  # Label X axis
```

This code produces Figure 16:

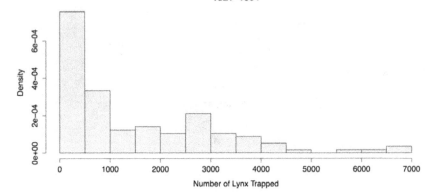

**Histogram of Annual Canadian Lynx Trappings
1821–1934**

Figure 16: *Modified Histogram*

Aside from the obvious changes of color and titles, there are two modifications to explain further. The **breaks** attribute sets the number of bins to use, but it is more a suggestion than other attributes. This means R will look at the suggestion but use its own algorithm to calculate bin width. I used an argument of 14 bins in this case, which is what R did, but I would still get 14 bins if I entered 11 here. R's autonomy in this respect may be an advantage, but if you want more control, you can set the breaks by hand. You can use a regular sequence to set the breaks at a uniform distance, like this: **breaks = seq(0, 7000, by = 100)**. You can also set each break by hand, like this: **breaks = c(0, 100, 300, 500, 3000, 3500, 7000)**. However, it's hard to imagine a situation where you would want to do that.

The other attribute I want to mention is **freq = FALSE**. By default, R labels the Y axis with bin frequencies. **freq = FALSE** changes the axis labels to density, or proportions. This does not change the shape of the distribution but it does allow one important addition. When the histogram is a density chart, it is possible to superimpose other distributions. It is then much easier to judge normality and identify important deviations.

In the code that follows I will add four plots to the histogram:

- A normal distribution.
- A kernel density estimate using the default bandwidth.
- A kernel density estimate using an adjusted bandwidth.
- A rug, or line plot, that appears underneath the distribution.

```
# SUPERIMPOSED NORMAL DISTRIBUTION
curve(dnorm(x, mean = mean(lynx), sd = sd(lynx)),  # Shape, mean, SD
      col = "thistle4",  # Color of the curve.
      lewd = 2,  # Line width of 2 pixels.
```

```
         add = TRUE)  # Superimpose on the previous graph.

# SUPERIMPOSED KERNEL DENSITY ESTIMATES
lines(density(lynx), col = "blue", lwd = 2)
lines(density(lynx, adjust = 3), col = "darkgreen", lwd = 2)

# SUPERIMPOSED RUG PLOT
rug(lynx, lwd = 2)
```

In this case, the **curve()** function calls for a **dnorm** distribution, or normal density distribution. (There are many other choices; see **?curve** for more.) The first line also uses two functions as arguments: **mean = mean(lynx)** and **sd = sd(lynx)**. These functions match the curve's mean and standard deviation to the histogram's. This shortcut saves effort and rounding error. The kernel density estimates work on the empirical data, so there is no need to adjust parameters other than bandwidth. (See **?kernel** for more.) The rug mirrors the distribution. The result is Figure 17:

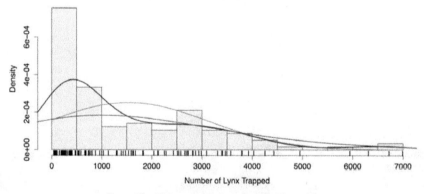

Histogram of Annual Canadian Lynx Trappings
1821–1934

Figure 17:   *Histogram with Superimposed Normal Curve*

Once you have saved your work, clean the workspace of unneeded variables and objects:

```
# CLEAN UP
detach("package:datasets", unload = TRUE)  # Unloads data sets package.
rm(list = ls())  # Remove all objects from workspace.
```

Boxplots

The last univariate chart we will discuss is the boxplot. Boxplots are well suited to identifying outliers in quantitative variables. The default boxplot is simple to create:

Sample: sample_2_5.R

```
# LOAD DATA SET
require("datasets")  # Load datasets package.
data(lynx)  # Annual Canadian Lynx trappings 1821-1934.
# BOXPLOT WITH DEFAULTS
boxplot(lynx)
```

This command produces the rudimentary boxplot in Figure 18:

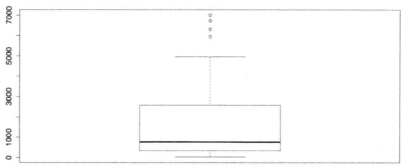

Figure 18: *Default Boxplot*

Figure 18 would be better if it had labels and if it were horizontal. There are also several other options for boxplots:

```
# BOXPLOT WITH OPTIONS
boxplot(lynx,
        horizontal = TRUE,  # Draw boxplot horizontally.
        las = 1,  # Make all labels horizontal.
        notch = TRUE,  # Notches for CI for median.
        col = "slategray3",   # Color for the central box.
        boxwex = 0.5,  # Width of box as proportion of original.
```

```
    whisklty = 1,  # Whisker line type; 1 = solid line
    staplelty = 0,  # Staple (line at end) type; 0 = none
    outpch = 16,  # Symbols for outliers; 16 = filled circle
    outcol = "slategray3",  # Color for outliers.
    main = "Histogram of Annual Canadian Lynx Trappings\n1821-1934",
    xlab = "Number of Lynx Trapped")  # Label the x-axis.
```

This produces the improved boxplot in Figure 19:

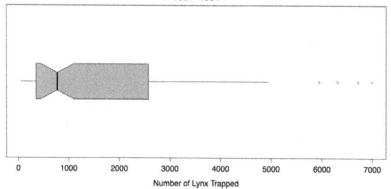

Boxplot of Annual Canadian Lynx Trappings
1821–1934

Number of Lynx Trapped

Figure 19: *Modified Boxplot*

The boxplot in Figure 19 emphasizes the asymmetry of the distribution as well as the gaps and outliers. This is important information for the statistical analyses, which is what we will discuss in the next chapter.

Once you have saved your work, you should clear the workspace of unneeded variables, objects, or packages:

```
# CLEAN UP
detach("package:datasets", unload = TRUE)  # Unloads data sets package.
rm(list = ls())  # Removes all objects from workspace.
```

Chapter 3 Statistics for One Variable

In Chapter 2 we examined graphs for one variable, which is the best beginning step for analyses. In Chapter 3, we will examine the follow-up to graphical analysis: statistical procedures for one variable.

Frequencies

As with the last chapter, we will begin with categorical variables. The most common statistics for categorical variables are frequencies and proportions. We will first create a data set based on a recent Google search.

Sample: sample_3_1.R

```
# ENTER DATA
# Hits in millions for each word on Google
groups <- c(rep("blue", 3990),
            rep("red", 4140),
            rep("orange", 1890),
            rep("green", 3770),
            rep("purple", 855))
```

The `rep()` function repeats an item for a specified number of times. In the above code, for example, it repeats the word "blue" 3990 times. When the five color words are put together in the object **groups**, there are 14,645 lines of data. Although it may be easier to work with the data in tabular form—which is what we will do—I prefer to also have a data set with one row per case.

This next command creates a data table:

```
# CREATE FREQUENCY TABLES
groups.t1 <- table(groups)  # Creates frequency table
groups.t1 # Print table
  blue  green orange purple    red
  3990   3770   1890    855   4140
```

The data are now in alphabetical order. There may be times when this is helpful, but for now it makes more sense to order them by frequencies.

```
# MODIFY FREQUENCY TABLES
groups.t2 <- sort(groups.t1, decreasing = TRUE)  # Sorts by frequency
groups.t2  # Prints table
groups
   red    blue   green orange purple
  4140    3990    3770   1890    855
```

You may also want to present the data as proportions or percentages instead of frequencies. The function **prop.table()** will do this:

```
# PROPORTIONS AND PERCENTAGES
prop.table(groups.t2)  # Gives proportions of the total.
      red       blue      green     orange     purple
0.2826903  0.2724479  0.2574257  0.1290543  0.0583817
```

There are too many decimal places in this table. We can fix this with the **round()** function. We place the **prop.table()** function inside it and specify the number of decimal places we want:

```
round(prop.table(groups.t2), 2)  # Round to 2 decimal places.
   red   blue  green orange purple
  0.28   0.27   0.26   0.13   0.06
```

That's an improvement but we can take it further. The leading zeroes and decimals are repetitive. We can remove them by multiplying the results by 100:

```
round(prop.table(groups.t2), 2) * 100  # Percents without decimals.
   red   blue  green orange purple
    28     27     26     13      6
```

Once you have saved your work, you should clear the workspace of unneeded variables and objects with **rm(list = ls())**.

Descriptive statistics

For categorical variables, there is a limited number of useful descriptive statistics. For quantitative variables, however, there is a much broader range of choices. In this section, we will use both R's built-in functions and functions from external packages. Together, they give a rich statistical picture of our data.

We will use R's data set **cars**, which gives the speed of cars in MPH and the distances taken to stop in feet. The data were recorded in the 1920s, so there are some unusual values, such as a car taking 120 feet to stop from 24 MPH. (See **?cars** for more information.)

Sample: sample_3_2.R

```
# LOAD DATA SET
require("datasets")  # Load the data sets package
cars  # Print the cars data to the console
data(cars)  # Load the data into the workspace
```

The easiest way to get descriptive statistics in R is with the **summary()** function. For quantitative variables, this function gives the five quartile values—minimum, first quartile, median, third quartile, and maximum—as well as the mean. It can also give some categorical statistics.

To get statistics for a single variable, enter the variable's name:

```
summary(cars$speed)  # Summary for one variable
   Min. 1st Qu.  Median    Mean 3rd Qu.    Max.
    4.0    12.0    15.0    15.4    19.0    25.0
```

You can also do an entire data set at once:

```
summary(cars)  # Summary for entire table (inc. categories)
     speed            dist
 Min.   : 4.0   Min.   :  2.00
 1st Qu.:12.0   1st Qu.: 26.00
 Median :15.0   Median : 36.00
 Mean   :15.4   Mean   : 42.98
 3rd Qu.:19.0   3rd Qu.: 56.00
 Max.   :25.0   Max.   :120.00
```

Another option for descriptive statistics is the **describe** function in the **psych** package. This provides the following:

- n
- mean
- standard deviation
- median
- trimmed mean (10% by default)

- median absolute deviation from median (MAD)
- minimum
- maximum
- range
- skewness
- kurtosis
- standard error

To use the describe function, you must first install and load the **psych** package, then call the **describe()** function:

```
# ALTERNATIVE DESCRIPTIVES
require("psych")
describe(cars)
        var  n  mean    sd median trimmed   mad
speed    1 50 15.40  5.29     15   15.47  5.93
dist     2 50 42.98 25.77     36   40.88 23.72
        min  max range  skew kurtosis   se
speed    4   25    21 -0.11    -0.67 0.75
dist     2  120   118  0.76     0.12 3.64
```

For more information on this package, enter **help(package = "psych")**. For help on the **describe()** function, enter **?describe**.

Once you have saved your work, you should clear the workspace of unneeded variables, objects, or packages:

```
# CLEAN UP
detach("package:datasets", unload = TRUE)  # Unloads data sets package.
detach("package:psych", unload=TRUE)  # Unloads psych package.
rm(list = ls())  # Remove all objects from workspace.
```

Single proportion: Hypothesis test and confidence interval

The simplest inferential procedures are for single proportions. These are dichotomous outcomes: pass or fail, yes or no, left or right, etc. The only data needed for these procedures is the number of trials, n, and the number of positive outcomes, X. For example, if a person flipped a coin 40 times and got 27 heads, then n = 40 and X = 27. R's **prop.test()** function is able to do both a null hypothesis test and a confidence interval for these proportions. We will use our coin flip data for this example, first with the default settings and then with some options.

Sample: sample_3_3.R

```
# PROPORTIONS TEST WITH DEFAULTS
prop.test(27, 40)  # 27 heads in 40 coin flips.
        1-sample proportions test with continuity correction
data:  27 out of 40, null probability 0.5
X-squared = 4.225, df = 1, p-value = 0.03983
alternative hypothesis: true p is not equal to 0.5
95 percent confidence interval:
 0.5075690 0.8092551
sample estimates:
    p
0.675
```

In these results, R repeats the data—27 positive outcomes out of 40 trials—and gives the default null probability of 0.5. "X-squared" is χ^2, the chi-squared value of 4.225. With one degree of freedom, our observed results have a probability value of 0.03983. Because this value is less than the standard .05, we reject the null hypothesis; that is, we conclude that 27 out of 40 heads is statistically significantly greater than 50%. R then states the alternative hypothesis that the true p, or the probability of a positive outcome, is not equal to 0.5. Next is the 95% confidence interval for the proportion, which ranges from 0.51 to 0.81. The output finishes with the observed sample proportion of 0.675, or 67.5%.

R also provides several options for the one-sample proportions test. These options include:

- The choice of a null proportion other than 0.5. non-directional, two-sided hypothesis test or a directional, one-sided test. In the latter case, you must specify whether you hypothesize that the sample proportion is greater than or less than the population value.
- The choice of a confidence level other than the default of 0.95.
- The choice of whether to use Yates' continuity correction; the default is to use it.

Using some of these options, we could revise the previous hypothesis test we conducted to test whether the sample proportion is significantly greater than a population proportion of 0.6 and we could use a confidence level of .90:

```
# PROPORTION TEST WITH OPTIONS

prop.test(27, 40,  # Same observed values.

          p = .6,  # Null probability of .6 (vs. .5).

          alt = "greater",  # Directional test for greater value.

          conf.level = .90)  # Confidence level of 90% (vs. 95%).


          1-sample proportions test with continuity correction

data:  27 out of 40, null probability 0.6
X-squared = 0.651, df = 1, p-value = 0.2099
alternative hypothesis: true p is greater than 0.6
90 percent confidence interval:
 0.5619655 1.0000000
sample estimates:

    p
0.675
```

While the sample proportion of 67.5% is the same as the default test, we are now using a population of 60%. Even with a directional hypothesis, the sample value does not differ significantly from the null value; with a p-value of 0.21, we cannot reject the null hypothesis. The confidence interval is interesting, too, because it is directional. As a result, the upper limit goes to 1.000, which it would not do for a standard, non-directional test.

Once you have saved your work, you should clear the workspace of unneeded variables and objects with rm(list = ls()).

Single mean: Hypothesis test and confidence interval

For quantitative variables—that is, variables at the interval or ratio level of measurement—the simplest possible test is the one-sample t-test. This test compares the sample mean to a hypothesized population mean.

In this example, we will use R's **quakes** data set. This data set includes the location, depth, and magnitude of earthquakes, as well as the number of measurement stations that detected the earthquake. It includes data for 1000 earthquakes off the coast of Fiji with a magnitude of at least 4.0 on the Richter scale.

We will examine one variable: **mag**, for magnitude. Before we conduct the t-test, though, we should at least get a histogram and some basic summary statistics.

Sample: sample_3_4.R

```
# LOAD DATA & EXAMINE
require("datasets")  # Loads data sets package.
 mag <- quakes$mag  # Loads just the magnitude variable.
hist(mag)
summary(mag)
```

The histogram in Figure 20 shows that the distribution has a strong, positive skew. The distribution is censored, with no values below 4.0, so it is difficult to know what the shape of the entire distribution would be.

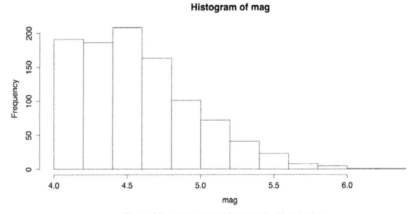

Histogram of mag

Figure 20: *Histogram of Earthquake Magnitudes*

The basic summary statistics for **mag** are:

Min.	1st Qu.	Median	Mean	3rd Qu.	Max.
4.00	4.30	4.60	4.62	4.90	6.40

The important value here is the mean of 4.62 because that is the value that the t-test compares against a hypothesized population mean.

The default t-test is simple to run:

```
# T-TEST WITH DEFAULTS
t.test(mag)
        One Sample t-test
data:  mag
t = 362.7599, df = 999, p-value < 2.2e-16
alternative hypothesis: true mean is not equal to 0
95 percent confidence interval:
 4.595406 4.645394
sample estimates:
mean of x
   4.6204
```

The output resembles that of the chi-squared test. It gives a t-value of 362.7599, which is enormous. The degrees of freedom are 999, and the probability value is almost zero: 2.2e-16. These strong results are not surprising, though; the hypothesized population mean was 0 but the lowest value in the data was 4. The output also includes the bounds for the 95% confidence interval and the observed sample mean.

Also like the chi-squared test, the t-test provides several options. (See ?t.test for more information.) The following t-test uses some of those options:

```
# T-TEST WITH OPTIONS
t.test(mag,
        alternative = "greater",  # Directional test
        mu = 4.5,                 # Null population mean of 4.5
        conf.level = 0.99)        # Confidence level of 99%


        One Sample t-test
data:  mag
t = 9.4529, df = 999, p-value < 2.2e-16
alternative hypothesis: true mean is greater than 4.5
99 percent confidence interval:
 4.590722      Inf
sample estimates:
mean of x
   4.6204
```

The conclusion here is matches the default t-test: the p-value is almost zero and we reject the null hypothesis. This is true even though we chose a hypothesized population mean—μ or mu—of 4.5, which was much closer to the sample mean of 4.62. The difference between the two means is much smaller than before but, given the large sample size of 1000, even negligible differences would be statistically significant.

Once you have saved your work, you should clear the workspace of unneeded variables, objects, or packages:

```
# CLEAN UP
detach("package:datasets", unload = TRUE)  # Unloads data sets package.
rm(list = ls())  # Remove all objects from workspace.
```

Chi-squared goodness-of-fit test

When you have a categorical variable with more than two categories, a chi-squared – χ^2 – test can be useful. In this section of the book we will talk about one variation of the chi-squared test: the goodness-of-fit test. This test compares the proportion of your sample in each category with hypothesized proportions. You can check if an equal number of your observations are in each category. (See ?chisq.test for more information.) That is the version of the test we will first cover. You can also check whether you observations match some other hypothesized distribution. We will cover that afterwards.

The chi-squared test in R uses summary tables as its input. If you have one row of data for each case or if you have a multidimensional table, you may need to restructure your data. In this example, we will use the three-dimensional table HairEyeColor from R's datasets package.

Sample: sample_3_5.R

```
# LOAD DATA & EXAMINE
require("datasets")  # Loads data sets package.
# SHOW DATA & MARGINAL FREQUENCIES
HairEyeColor  # Shows data; see ?HairEyeColor for more information.
margin.table(HairEyeColor, 1)  # Hair color marginal frequencies.
margin.table(HairEyeColor, 2)  # Eye color marginal frequencies.
margin.table(HairEyeColor, 3)  # Sex marginal frequencies.
margin.table(HairEyeColor)     # Total frequencies.
```

You can see the full, three-way table by entering ?HairEyeColor. In this analysis, though, we will look only at eye color, so we should create a new data frame to hold those data.

```
# CREATE DATA FRAME
eyes <- margin.table(HairEyeColor, 2)  # Save the table.
eyes  # Show frequency table in the console.
Brown  Blue Hazel Green
  220   215   93    64


round(prop.table(eyes), 2)  # Proportions w/2 digits
Brown  Blue Hazel Green
 0.37  0.36  0.16  0.11
```

We will first conduct a version of the chi-squared goodness-of-fit test with the hypothesis that the eye colors are evenly distributed. This is the default setting for **chisq.test()**.

```
# CHI-SQUARED GOODNESS-OF-FIT 1
# DEFAULT: EQUAL FREQUENCIES
chi1 <- chisq.test(eyes)  # Save test as object "chi1"
chi1  # Check results.
        Chi-squared test for given probabilities
data:  eyes
X-squared = 133.473, df = 3, p-value < 2.2e-16
```

The chi-squared test statistic, shown as X-squared in R's printout, is enormous: 133.473. With three degrees of freedom, the test result has a probability value of nearly zero. Because this probability value is less than the conventional cut-off of .06—much less, in fact—we reject the null hypothesis that the four eye colors are equally common among our sample.

This is, however, not the most appropriate test. Eye colors are not evenly distributed. A better test would be whether our sample proportions differ significantly from the population proportions for eye colors. R does not provide this population data, but the Internet does. One website[9] suggested that the population proportions for brown, blue, hazel, and green eyes were .41, .32, .14, and .12, respectively.[10] We can then combine these values in a vector of probability values using the p attribute in **chisq.test()** and see if there is a significant difference.

```
# CHI-SQUARED GOODNESS-OF-FIT 2
# OPTION: SPECIFY FREQUENCIES
```

---

[9] http://www.statisticbrain.com/eye-color-distribution-percentages
[10] If categories are combined to match R's four categories: Irises with specks and dark brown irises are combined with brown; blue/grey irises are combined with blue; blue/grey/green irises with brown/yellow specks are combined with hazel, and green/light brown irises with minimal specks are combined with green.

```
chi2 <- chisq.test(eyes, p = c(.41, .32, .15, .12))
chi2  # Check results
        Chi-squared test for given probabilities
data:  eyes
X-squared = 6.4717, df = 3, p-value = 0.09079
```

In this case our value of chi-square—again, X-squared in the printout—is much smaller: 6.4717. With three degrees of freedom, that gives a probability value of .09079, which does not exceed the standard cut-off of 0.5. We can therefore conclude that our sample's eye color proportions do *not* differ significantly from those of the general population.

At the end, we should clear the workspace of unneeded variables, objects, or packages:

```
# CLEAN UP
detach("package:datasets", unload = TRUE)  # Unloads data sets package.
rm(list = ls())  # Remove all objects from workspace.
```

Chapter 4   Modifying Data

I believe that all data can tell an attentive analyst *something* of worth. The problem is that the story you are able to get from the data may not be the story that you need. One method for getting results that are more closely aligned to your research questions can be to modify the data. In this chapter, we will discuss four kinds of modifications that can help you get more insights out of your data: compensating for outliers, transforming distributions, creating composite variables, and dealing with missing data.

Outliers

Outliers can distort analyses so much that the results are either misleading or meaningless. There are several common methods for dealing with outliers:

- **Leave them in.** If they are legitimate values and a necessary part of your equations, such as calculating the value of a stock portfolio, then they should remain.
- **Delete them.** If your goal is to analyze common cases, then it may be acceptable to delete outliers. Be clear that you have done so and give your justification.
- **Transform the data.** For example, with high outliers, it may help to use a logarithmic transformation. Again, be clear that you have done so and give your justification.
- **Use robust statistics.** Measures such as the mean, the trimmed mean, or various robust estimators are less affected by outliers. These measures are, however, more difficult to implement and do not correspond to other common analyses such as regression or correlation.

In this section we will look at the simplest of these adjustments: deleting outliers. We will use the `islands` data set from the R **data sets** package. This data set contains the areas of 48 landmasses that exceed 10,000 square miles. Several of these measurements are outliers.

The easiest way to check for outliers is with a boxplot, using R's **boxplot()** function, and then follow up with numerical descriptions from **boxplot.stats()**.

Sample: sample_4_1.R

```
# LOAD DATA & INITIAL CHECKS
require("datasets")
data(islands)  # Areas (in 1k sq mi) of landmasses > 10k sq mi (n = 48)
boxplot(islands, horizontal = TRUE)  # Many high outliers.
boxplot.stats(islands)  # Numbers for the boxplot.
```

Figure 21 shows that there are numerous outliers in this data set. In fact, the outliers comprise almost the entire range of measurements.

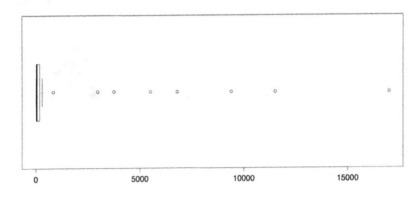

Figure 21: *Boxplot of Island Areas (in 1000 square miles)*

The **boxplot.stats()** function gives the five values for the boxplot's hinges (not including the outliers), as well as the sample size, the confidence intervals for the median,[11] and the values for the outliers. In this data set, the value for the upper fence is 306[12] and the closest outlier is 840. To delete the outliers, simply select all of the values beneath them. You can create a new data set with those values and then check the new distribution with this code:

```
# DELETE OUTLIERS
islands.low <- islands[islands < 500]  # Delete 8 highest
boxplot(islands.low, horizontal = TRUE)
boxplot.stats(islands.low)
```

Figure 22 shows the new boxplot for the reduced data set:

---

[11] The confidence interval for the median is calculated as +/-1.58 IQR/sqrt(n). See ?**boxplot.stats** for more information.

[12] Strangely, R labels this island as "Asia," which is not correct. It should say "New Guinea." The other labels are correct. The reason for the switch is not clear.

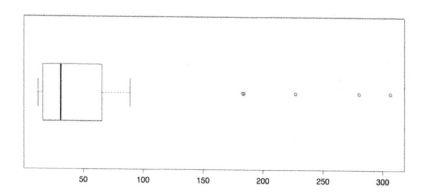

Figure 22: *Boxplot of Island Areas (8 Largest Deleted)*

It may be surprising that there are five new outliers in this distribution. That is because we deleted about 16% of the previous distribution, which adjusted the quartile values that are used in determining outliers. It is, of course, possible to repeat the process until there are no longer any outliers. Such an approach, though, if done without a sound theoretical justification,[13] does damage to the analysis. Such ad hoc approaches should be avoided as a rule.

Once you have saved your work, you should clear the workspace of unneeded variables, objects, or packages:

```
# CLEAN UP
detach("package:datasets", unload = TRUE)  # Unloads data sets package.
rm(list = ls())  # Remove all objects from the workspace.
```

Transformations

When we were confronted with outliers in the previous section, we simply deleted them. While this may be an expedient approach, it also loses data and may lead to distorted conclusions. Another way to way to deal with outliers is to transform the distribution. For example, in a distribution that has all positive scores and high outliers, a logarithmic transformation is often effective. This is the approach we will use for the `islands` data. If the data are still loaded from the previous exercise then we can go straight to the transformation.

Sample: sample_4_2.R

---

[13] There is, in fact, a theoretical justification for deleting the highest seven outliers from the original data set. This justification will be discussed in the section on dichotomization.

```
# LOGARITHMIC TRANSFORMATION
islands.ln <- log(islands)  # Compute natural log (base = e)
boxplot(islands.ln, horizontal = TRUE)  # Almost looks normal.
```

The `log()` function calculates natural logs with base e, which is approximately 2.718. R will also calculate common, base 10 logs with `log10()` and binary, base 2 logs with `log2()`, with similar results. (Note that is logarithms are undefined for zero. If you have zeros in your data, then you could add a small amount—0.5 or 1.0—to each score to avoid this problem.)

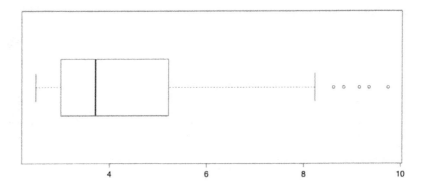

Figure 23: *Boxplot of Log Transformed Islands Data*

The boxplot of transformed values in Figure 23 has only a few outliers. It is also much better suited for analysis than the distribution of raw scores in Figure 21 or even the trimmed distribution in Figure 22.

A logarithmic transformation is not linear because it affects outlying scores more than central scores. It is, however, an information-preserving or reversible transformation. That is, it is possible to undo the transformation—by raising the scores to the appropriate exponent—and accurately recreate the original data. The next two transformations, by contrast, lose information. Each has its place, though, and can be useful depending on the nature of the data and the analytical question.

The first of these information-losing transformations is ranking. The scores are placed an order and a rank of 1 is given to either the highest or lowest score. The order of scores is maintained but the distance between scores is lost. One important consideration is how to deal with tied scores. R gives choices of "average," "first," "random," "max," and "min" (see **?rank** for more information). If random is used, then the histogram of scores is flat, as each score occurs only once.

```
# RANK TRANSFORMATION
islands.rank <- rank(islands, ties.method = "random")  # Ranks islands
```

The last method of data transformation that we will address is dichotomization, or splitting scores into two categories, such as high and low. This transformation loses the most information of all but can be useful for strongly skewed distributions with justifiable or naturally occurring breaks. In the islands data, there is such a naturally occurring split: out of the eight outlying scores, seven are continents. It is reasonable to separate continents from islands and so a dichotomous split may be appropriate. All that is needed is a command that assigns a score of 0 to any case with a value below a certain cutoff and a score of 1 to any case that is above the cutoff. In this data set, the largest island, Greenland, has an area of 804 (that is, 804,000 square miles), while the smallest continent, Australia, has an area of 2968, or nearly three million square miles. As such, any value between those two could serve as a cutoff. In the code below, a score of 1000 serves as the cutoff.

As a note, while the dichotomization can be done with a pair of if statements or an if and else, it is slightly more concise to use an ifelse statement (see ?ifelse). This function takes three arguments:

1. The test, islands > 1000 in this case.
2. The value to return if the test result is positive, 1 in this case.
3. The value to return if the test result is negative, 0 in this case.

The function then feeds into a new variable called continent, and assigns a 1 to all of the continents and a 0 to all of the islands. In this example, I also list all of the continents by using the command continent[continent == 1] , which says to print out the all of the rows of continent where the value for continent is equal to 1.

```
# DICHOTOMIZATION
continent <- ifelse(islands > 1000, 1, 0)  # Creates the indicator variable.
continent  # List islands and 0/1 for continent.
continent[continent == 1]  # List just the continents.
      Africa     Antarctica          Asia      Australia         Europe
           1              1             1              1              1
North America South America
           1              1
```

Each of these four transformations can be appropriate depending on your data and your research questions. The most important criterion when choosing a method is whether it is informative for your purposes, which is an important analytical judgment call.

Once you have saved your work, you should clear the workspace of unneeded variables, objects, or packages:

```
# CLEAN UP
detach("package:datasets", unload = TRUE)  # Unloads data sets package.
rm(list = ls())  # Remove all objects from workspace.
```

Composite variables

A common task in analytics is to create composite variables, or variables that are composed of other variables. Frequent examples include sums, averages, or weighted index scores. R has two built-in functions that make the first two of these tasks easy: rowSum() and rowMeans(). An unfortunate requirement of these functions, though, is that the entire data set must consist of numeric values and all of the variables must be included in order. (This stands in contrast to programs like SPSS or even Excel, which allow you to pick and choose variables as well as the order in which they are entered.) The solution to this problem is to create a sub-data frame that contains just the variables you need, as shown in the code that follows. We will begin by entering a small data set with three numeric variables and one string variable.

Sample: sample_4_3.R

```
# ENTER DATA
data1 <- read.table(
        header = TRUE, # First row is the header.
        # No comments within the data.
        text = '
        A  B  C   D
        5  3  1  D1
        2  4  6  D2
        6  7  8  D3
        ')
data1  # check data
```

The rowSum() and rowMeans() functions cannot include the string variable, so we can create a second data set that does not include it:

```
# CREATE DATA FRAME WITH NUMERIC VARIABLES ONLY
data2 <- data1[, 1:3]  # Exclude the string variable.
data2  # Check the data.
```

It is also possible to skip intermediate variables by using the concatenate function, c(). For example, if there were seven variables and we wanted to include variables 1, 2, 3, 5, and 7, but with 7 first, we could write data[, c(7, 1:3, 5)].

Once we have this reduced, numeric-variables-only data set, we can run the rowSum() and rowMeans() functions. Here is the first:

```
# AVERAGE ACROSS BOTH VARIABLES
# ROW SUMS
rowSums(data2)
[1]  9 12 21
```

And here is the second:

```
# ROW MEANS
rowMeans(data2)
[1] 3 4 7
```

Other arithmetic functions are possible if they are performed before creating the secondary data frame. Once you have saved your work, you should clear the workspace of unneeded variables and objects:

```
# CLEAN UP
rm(list = ls())  # Remove all objects from workspace.
```

Missing data

Missing data can present a substantial challenge for analysis. In R, missing data are typically coded as NA, for "not available."[14] Certain functions in R are able to accommodate missing data but others are not. For this reason, it is helpful to know how to deal with missing data. There are generally two approaches: remove or ignore the missing data, or replace the missing values with valid values through imputation.

Sample: sample_4_4.R

```
# DATA WITH NA
x1 <- c(1, 2, 3, NA, 5)  # Sample data with NA
```

---

[14] Another code is available, NaN for "not a number," but that doesn't usually apply to most missing data situations. For more information on both codes, see ?NA and ?NaN, respectively.

```
summary(x1)  # "summary" still works with NA
   Min. 1st Qu.  Median  Mean 3rd Qu.   Max.   NA's
   1.00   1.75    2.50   2.75   3.50    5.00      1
mean(x1)  # But "mean" doesn't
[1] NA
```

In the previous example, R's summary() function is able to work with missing data, but the closely related function mean() is not. If any values are NA for mean(), then the returned value is also NA.

In a large data set, it may not be obvious which cases are missing data. A combination of R functions, which() and is.na(), can give the index number for any NA values in the specified variable.

```
# FIND NA
which(is.na(x1))  # Gives index number of NA
[1] 4
```

It is possible to tell R to ignore NA values in certain functions, such as mean(), by including na.rm = TRUE.

```
# REMOVE NA
mean(x1, na.rm = TRUE)  # Removes NA from calculations
[1] 2.75
```

In other situations, especially multivariate analyses, it may be more helpful to replace missing values with other, valid values. This can be done with is.na() and a value to be assigned in the place of missing values, such as 0.

```
# REPLACE NA 1: IS.NA
x2 <- x1  # Copies data to new object
x2[is.na(x2)] <- 0  # If item in x2 is NA, replace with 0
x2  # Show revised data
[1] 1 2 3 0 5
```

A better approach to replacing missing values is to use the mean or some other value. This approach, known as imputation, can be implemented with the previous code by replacing the 0 in x2[is.na(x2)] <- 0 with mean(x2, na.rm = TRUE). (This requires that the original variable be copied first.) It is also possible to create a new variable and impute the mean with a single ifelse() command:

```
# REPLACE NA 2: IFELSE
x3 <- ifelse(is.na(x1), mean(x1, na.rm = TRUE), x1)   # Impute mean
x3   # Show revised data
[1] 1.00 2.00 3.00 2.75 5.00
```

These are a few very basic approaches to dealing with missing data. The treatment of missing data is an active area of research and many packages have been developed for this in R. Because these packages are updated or released frequently, I encourage you to look at R's official CRAN website or the third-party CRANtastic.

And finally, once you have saved your work, you should clear the workspace of unneeded variables and objects with rm(list = ls()).

Chapter 5 Working with the Data File

The univariate graphs and statistical procedures that we discussed in Chapters 2 and 3, as well as the methods for modifying data from Chapter 4, can suggest important ways to focus your analysis. Three of the most important methods of focusing include selecting subgroups for individual analysis, comparing subgroups, and integrating additional data—either new cases or new variables—into your data set. We will discuss each of those methods in this chapter.

Selecting cases

When you are working with your data, you may want to focus on certain subgroups of cases or variables to get better insight. R makes it simple to select cases and variables. The general syntax is this: `data set[rows, columns]` or `data set[cases, variables]`. To select all of the rows or columns, just leave the attribute empty. To select an adjacent set of cases or variables, give the index number of the first and last items with a colon between them. For example, this command would select rows 10-20 and columns 2-5: `data set[10:20, 2:5]`. To select nonadjacent cases or variables, use the concatenate function, `c()`. For example, to select all of the cases but just variables 1-4, 6, and 8-12, use this command: `data set[, c(1:4, 6, 8:12)]`.

In this example we will use the mtcars data from R's `datasets` package. This data set contains road test data from a 1974 issue of *Motor Trend* magazine. In the code that follows, we first load the package and the data, and then display the first three cases:

Sample: sample_5_1.R

```
# LOAD DATA

require("datasets")  # Load datasets package.

data(mtcars)  # 1974 road test data from Motor Trend.

mtcars[1:3, ]  # Show all variables for the first three cars.
               mpg cyl disp  hp drat    wt  qsec vs am gear carb
Mazda RX4      21.0   6  160 110 3.90 2.620 16.46  0  1    4    4
Mazda RX4 Wag  21.0   6  160 110 3.90 2.875 17.02  0  1    4    4
Datsun 710     22.8   4  108  93 3.85 2.320 18.61  1  1    4    1
```

Next, we'll get the mean horsepower for all of the cars in the data set. The only thing to remember in this command is how to specify a single variable in a data set with the `$` operator. In this way, the horsepower variable is `mtcars$hp`.

```
# ALL CASES
mean(mtcars$hp)  # Mean horsepower for all cars.
[1] 146.6875
```

Now we'll get the mean horsepower for just the eight cylinder cars. Put the name of the selection variable in square brackets and use the double equal signs, ==, which indicate logical equality.

```
# SELECT ON SINGLE VARIABLE
# Mean horsepower (for 8-cylinder cars).
mean(mtcars$hp[mtcars$cyl == 8])  # Select rows where cyl = 8
[1] 209.2143
```

If you plan on doing several analyses with the same subgroup, it may be helpful to create a new data frame based on that selection. In that case, make the selection and assign it to a new variable. In the following code I create a data frame called **v8** for all the eight cylinder cars. The first part of the selection in square brackets selects the rows for cars with eight cylinder engines and the blank space after the comma selects all of the variables.

```
# CREATE NEW DATA FRAME WITH SELECTION
v8 <- mtcars[mtcars$cyl == 8, ]  # 8-cylinder cars, all variables
```

Using the new data frame, I can now select on two other variables: cars with 5-speed transmission and cars that weigh less than 4000 pounds. The average horsepower for this group is 299.5, which is very high for 1974, so I followed up by listing all of the cars that met these criteria and selecting a few variables to display.

```
# SELECT ON TWO VARIABLES
# Mean horsepower for cars with v8, 5-speed, and weigh < 4000 lbs.
mean(v8$hp[v8$gear == 5 & v8$wt < 4])  # Show the mean horsepower.
[1] 299.5
v8[v8$gear == 5 & v8$wt < 4, c(2, 10, 6, 4)]  # List the cars included.
                cyl gear   wt  hp
Ford Pantera L    8    5 3.17 264
Maserati Bora     8    5 3.57 335
```

Only two cars made this list: the De Tomaso Pantera (incorrectly listed here as a Ford, although it had a Ford engine[15]) and the Maserati Bora.

Once you have saved your work, you should clear the workspace of unneeded variables, objects, or packages:

```
# CLEAN UP
detach("package:datasets", unload = TRUE)  # Unloads data sets package.
rm(list = ls())  # Remove all objects from workspace.
```

Analyzing by subgroups

In the last section we looked methods to select subgroups for analysis at the exclusion of other groups. In this section we will look at methods to include all of the cases in the analyses but to organize the results by subgroups.

In this example, we will use the Iris data set[16] that was collected by botanist Edgar Anderson but made famous by statistician Ronald Fisher. This data set consists of four measurements for three species of Iris. We will compare the three species.

Sample: sample_5_2.R

```
# LOAD DATA
require("datasets")  # Load the data sets package.


# PREVIEW DATA
iris[1:3, ]  # Show first three rows, all variables.
  Sepal.Length Sepal.Width Petal.Length Petal.Width Species
1          5.1         3.5          1.4         0.2  setosa
2          4.9         3.0          1.4         0.2  setosa
3          4.7         3.2          1.3         0.2  setosa
```

For this example, we will compare the petal widths of the three species. To do this, we will use the **aggregate()** function, which is used to compute summary statistics for subgroups. (See **?aggregate** for more information.) The function takes three arguments:

1. The variable to be analyzed. In this case, **iris$Petal.Width**.

---

[15] See http://en.wikipedia.org/wiki/De_Tomaso_Pantera
[16] See **?iris** or http://en.wikipedia.org/wiki/Iris_flower_data_set for more information.

2. The variable that specified group membership. In this case, **iris$Species**.
3. The function or statistics to be used. In this case, **FUN = mean**.

The tilde operator, ~, is used to separate the left and right sides of a model formula. R organizes the output like this:

```
# COMPARE GROUPS ON ONE VARIABLE
aggregate(iris$Petal.Width ~ iris$Species, FUN = mean)
  iris$Species iris$Petal.Width
1       setosa            0.246
2   versicolor            1.326
3    virginica            2.026
```

To compare the groups on more than one outcome variable, replace the single outcome variable with the column binding function **cbind()** and list the desired outcomes as arguments. **cbind()** makes it possible to combine several vectors or variables into a single, new data frame. (Enter **?cbind** for more information.) In this case, R does not give the variable names but uses generic labels—**V1, V2**, etc.—so you must note the order in which you entered the variables.

```
# COMPARE GROUPS ON TWO VARIABLES
aggregate(cbind(iris$Petal.Width,
                iris$Petal.Length)
          ~ iris$Species,
          FUN = mean)
  iris$Species    V1    V2
1       setosa 0.246 1.462
2   versicolor 1.326 4.260
3    virginica 2.026 5.552
```

Once you have saved your work, you should clean the workspace by removing any variables or objects you created.

```
# CLEAN UP
detach("package:datasets", unload = TRUE)  # Unloads data sets package.
rm(list = ls())  # Remove all objects from workspace.
```

Merging files

Analyses are often much more powerful if data from different sources are combined. For example, joining data on Internet search trends with data on demographics can give important insights for marketing researchers. In this section, we will examine the **longley** data from R's **datasets** package. This is a data frame with seven economic variables, observed yearly from 1947 to 1962. (See **?longley** for more information.) After loading the data and displaying a few cases, we will then split the data set into three parts and then join them again to demonstrate the process.

Sample: sample_5_3.R

```
# LOAD DATA
require("datasets")   # Load the data sets package.
# DISPLAY DATA
longley[1:3, ]  # Display the first three rows, all variables.
      GNP.deflator      GNP Unemployed Armed.Forces Population Year Employed
1947          83.0  234.289      235.6        159.0    107.608 1947   60.323
1948          88.5  259.426      232.5        145.6    108.632 1948   61.122
1949          88.2  258.054      368.2        161.6    109.773 1949   60.171
```

Now we will split the data into three data sets. First, we will create a data set called **a1** with the first six of seven variables for the first 14 of 16 cases. Second, we will create another data set called **a2,** which will have the last two of seven variables for the same 14 cases. This means that data sets **a1** and **a2** will share one variable: **year**. This variable will serve as the index variable that makes it possible to line up cases when adding variables. The third data set, called **b**, will have all seven variables but will add two new cases.

Although it is not necessary to first save the data sets as new objects in the workspace, it is a convenient way of checking the process. After the data sets have been created, we will then use **write.table()** to save them as text files on the host computer. To do so, we provide the name of the object to be written and its file path. The file path specification works slightly differently on Macintosh and Windows PCs. On my Mac, I would write **"~/Desktop/longley.a1.txt"** to save the file to my desktop. On a Windows PC, I would write **"c:/longley.a1.txt"** to save the file to the C drive. It is also important to specify that values in the table are separated by tabs by adding **sep = "\t"**. Once everything has been written correctly, then we can use **rm(list=ls())** to clear the workspace and start the imports with a clean space.

```
# SPLIT & EXPORT DATA
a1 <- longley[1:14, 1:6]  # First 14 cases, first 6 variables.
a2 <- longley[1:14, 6:7]  # First 14 cases, last 2 variables.
b <- longley[15:16, ]     # Last 2 cases, all variables.
```

```
write.table(a1, "~/Desktop/longley.a1.txt", sep = "\t")
write.table(a2, "~/Desktop/longley.a2.txt", sep = "\t")
write.table(b, "~/Desktop/longley.b.txt", sep = "\t")
# On PC, use "c:/longley.a1.txt"
rm(list=ls()) # Clear out everything to start fresh
```

Once all of the data files have been exported and the workspace has been cleaned, we can start over by importing them one at a time and putting them together. We'll start by importing and combining the two data sets with the variables for the first 14 cases: **a1**, which has the first six variables (including **year**), and **a2**, which has the last two variables (also including **year**). To do this we use **read.table()** to import the data sets. Then we use **merge()** to match the cases in the data sets. **merge()** takes three arguments:

1. The name of the first data set.
2. The name of the second data set.
3. The variable used to match cases, with the argument **by**.

In this example, I feed the merge into a new object **a.1.2** and then display the first few cases to check the outcome.

```
# IMPORT & COMBINE FIRST TWO DATA SETS
# Add columns for same cases.
a1t <- read.table("~/Desktop/longley.a1.txt", sep = "\t")
a2t <- read.table("~/Desktop/longley.a2.txt", sep = "\t")
# Take early years (a1t) and add columns (a2t).
# Must specify the variable to match cases ("Year" in this case).
a.1.2 <- merge(a1t, a2t, by = "Year")   # Merge two data frames
a.1.2[1:3, ]   # Check results for the first three cases.
  Year GNP.deflator     GNP Unemployed Armed.Forces Population Employed
1 1947        83.0 234.289      235.6        159.0    107.608   60.323
2 1948        88.5 259.426      232.5        145.6    108.632   61.122
3 1949        88.2 258.054      368.2        161.6    109.773   60.171
```

Notice addition of the index variable on left, numbered **1, 2, 3**. In the original data set the index variable was the year of the observation, with **year** also appearing as the sixth variable. In the new data set, **year** was used to match observations and so it now appears as the first variable.

To add the new cases from the data set b, first we import the data set with **read.table()**. Then we use the row binding function **rbind()** to join the two data sets. What's interesting is that this works even though the variables are currently in a different order, with **year** moving to the front on the first data set.

```
# IMPORT & COMBINE LAST DATA SET
# Add two more cases at the bottom.
b <- read.table("~/Desktop/longley.b.txt", sep = "\t")
all.data <- rbind(a.1.2, b)  # "Row Bind"
all.data[12:16, ]  # Check last four rows, all variables.
     Year GNP.deflator     GNP Unemployed Armed.Forces Population Employed
13   1959        112.6 482.704      381.3        255.2    123.366   68.655
14   1960        114.2 502.601      393.1        251.4    125.368   69.564
1961 1961        115.7 518.173      480.6        257.2    127.852   69.331
1962 1962        116.9 554.894      400.7        282.7    130.081   70.551
```

There is one problem with this process. Notice the mismatch of index variables on the left of the previous output. We can fix this by resetting the row names with **row.names() <- NULL**, making sure to insert the name of the data set, as shown in the following code:

```
# CLEAN DATA
row.names(all.data) <- NULL  # Reset row names.
all.data[13:16, ]  # Check last four rows, all variables.
   Year GNP.deflator     GNP Unemployed Armed.Forces Population Employed
13 1959        112.6 482.704      381.3        255.2    123.366   68.655
14 1960        114.2 502.601      393.1        251.4    125.368   69.564
15 1961        115.7 518.173      480.6        257.2    127.852   69.331
16 1962        116.9 554.894      400.7        282.7    130.081   70.551
```

At this point, the three data sets have been successfully joined and we can proceed with our analyses. And, as before, once we have saved our work, we should clean the workspace by removing any variables or objects we created.

```
# CLEAN UP
detach("package:datasets", unload = TRUE)  # Unloads data sets package.
rm(list = ls())  # Remove all objects from workspace.
```

Chapter 6 Charts for Associations

I mentioned in the Preface to this book my belief that graphics should always come before statistical analyses. The graphics can provide vital context and insight to the analyses that could be easily lost if the statistical procedures came first. Accordingly, in the chapters on univariate analyses, we first discussed charts for one variable (see Chapter 2) and then statistics for one variable (see Chapter 3). We continue that pattern for bivariate associations, with charts for association here in Chapter 6, and statistics for association in Chapter 7.

Grouped bar charts of frequencies

When a data set consists of joint categorizations based on two variables, grouped bar charts of the joint frequencies are often the most informative graph. In this section, we begin by entering a small 2 x 3 table of data directly into R. This is done by nesting the **read.table()** function within the **as.matrix()** function. We have to convert the data to a matrix since the plotting functions that we will use expect the data to be in vectors or matrices. In addition, two attributes are specified: **header** = TRUE, which indicates that the first row of data contains the names for the levels on the first categorical variable, and **row.names** = 1, which indicates that the first column contains the names for the levels on the second categorical variables. The data themselves consist of the frequencies for each combination of levels.

Sample: sample_6_1.R

```
# ENTER DATA
data1 <- as.matrix(read.table(    # Save as matrix
         header = TRUE,  # First row is the header.
         row.names = 1,  # First column is row names.
         # No comments within the data.
         text = '
         X  A  B  C
         L  5  3  1
         R  2  4  6
         '))
data1  # Check the data.
```

The next step is to create the barplot using R's **barplot()** function. The most important part of this command is the attribute **beside** = TRUE, which places the bars side-by-side instead of stacked.

```
# CREATE BARPLOT
barplot(data1,  # Use a new summary table.
        beside = TRUE,  # Bars side-by-side vs. stacked.
        col = c("steelblue3", "thistle3"),  # Colors
        main = "Side by Side Barplots",
        xlab = "Groups",
        ylab = "frequency")
```

It is possible to add a legend as an attribute in the **barplot()** command. However, an interesting alternative is to add the legend interactively. By first making the plot with the previous code and then executing the following code, the cursor changes to crosshairs and allows you to manually position the legend within the plot:

```
# ADD LEGEND INTERACTIVELY
legend(locator(1),  # Use mouse to locate the legend.
       rownames(data1),  # Use matrix row names (A & B).
       fill = c("steelblue3", "thistle3"))  # Colors
```

The resulting grouped bar plot is shown in Figure 24.

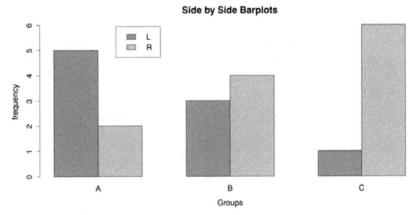

Figure 24: *Grouped Bar Chart for Frequencies*

As usual, once you have saved your work, you should clean the workspace by removing any variables or objects you created with **rm(list = ls())**.

Bar charts of group means

When data consist of quantitative data for several groups on a single categorical variable, then a bar chart of group means can be helpful. To create this chart in R, it is necessary to reorganize the raw data into a table of means, which can then be charted with the same `barplot()` function that we used in the last section. In this example we will use the `InsectSprays` data from R's `datasets` package.

Sample: sample_6_2.R

```
# LOAD DATA
require("datasets")  # Load the datasets package.
spray <- InsectSprays  # Load data with shorter name.
```

In order to make a bar chart of means, we first need to save the means into their own object. We can do this with the `aggregate()` function, in which the outcome variable `spray$count` is a function of `spray$spray` and `FUN = mean` requests the means.

```
# GET GROUP MEANS
means <- aggregate(spray$count ~ spray$spray, FUN = mean)
means  # Check the data.
```

The resulting data frame `means` consists of a column of index values and a column of means. We need to remove the column of names and transpose the means. We can do this with the transpose function `t()` and the argument `[-1]`, which excludes the first column. We then put the group names back in as column names with the `colnames()` function and specifying `mean[, 1]`, which calls for all rows of the first column. The transposed data and columns names are saved into a new object, `mean.data`.

```
# REORGANIZE DATA FOR BARPLOT
mean.data <- t(means[-1])  # Removes the first column, transposes the second.
colnames(mean.data) <- means[, 1]  # Add group names as column names.
mean.data
```

Once the data have been rearranged in this manner, all that remains is to call the `barplot()` function.

```
# BARPLOT WITH DEFAULTS
barplot(mean.data)
```

It is, however, useful to add some options to `barplot()`, especially to add titles and labels.

```
# BARPLOT WITH OPTIONS
barplot(mean.data,
        col  = "red",
        main = "Effectiveness of Insect Sprays",
        xlab = "Spray Used",
        ylab = "Insect Count")
```

This will produce the chart shown in Figure 25.

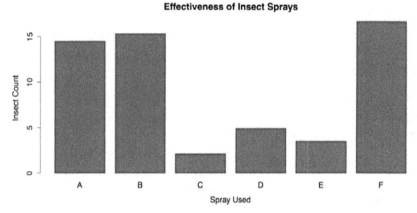

Effectiveness of Insect Sprays

Figure 25: *Bar Chart of Group Means*

Finish by cleaning the workspace and removing any variables or objects you created.

```
# CLEAN UP
detach("package:datasets", unload = TRUE)  # Unloads the datasets package.
rm(list = ls())  # Remove all objects from workspace.
```

Grouped box plots

In the last section we looked at bar charts for group means. While such a chart can be useful, it only shows one piece of data, the mean, for each group. It may also be important to look at the entire distribution of scores for each group. This would allow you to check for outliers by group as well as get an intuitive feel for how well your data meet statistical assumptions like homogeneity of variance.

For this example, we will use the **painters** data set from the **MASS** package.[17] This data set contains 18th century art critic Roger de Piles' judgments of 54 classical painters on four characteristics: composition, drawing, color, and expression.[18] The painters are classified according to their "school." This is indicated by a factor level code as follows: "A": Renaissance; "B": Mannerist; "C": Seicento; "D": Venetian; "E": Lombard; "F": Sixteenth Century; "G": Seventeenth Century; "H": French. These classifications form the basis of our analysis.

Sample: sample_6_3.R

```
# LOAD DATA
# Use data set "painters" from the package "MASS"
require("MASS")
data(painters)
painters[1:3, ]
          Composition Drawing Colour Expression School
Da Udine           10       8     16          3      A
Da Vinci           15      16      4         14      A
Del Piombo          8      13     16          7      A
```

The data set is well formatted and ready for use with R's **boxplot()** function. All that is necessary is to specify the outcome variable and categorizing variable. In this case, these are **painters$Expression** and **painters$School**, respectively.

```
# GROUPED BOXPLOTS WITH DEFAULTS
# Draw boxplots of outcome (Expression) by group (School)
boxplot(painters$Expression ~ painters$School)
```

The default boxplot produced by this code is displayed in Figure 26.

---

[17] This package includes functions and data sets that are included in *Modern Applied Statistics with S*, a 2002 textbook by Venables and Ripley. See **help(package = "MASS")** for more information.

[18] For an interesting follow-up on this data, see "Taste Endures! The Rankings of Roger de Piles (†1709) and Three Centuries of Art Prices" by Kathryn Graddy at http://people.brandeis.edu/~kgraddy/published%20papers/DePiles_complete.pdf.

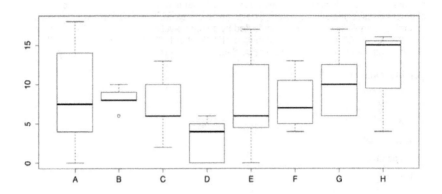

Figure 26: *Grouped Boxplots (Default Chart)*

As a chart, Figure 26 has one glaring omission: the groups do not have meaningful labels. Instead, they are categorized as A, B, C, and so on. This defeats the purpose of the chart. Consequently, it is important to add those labels using the **names()** attribute. It is also a good idea to add titles, axis labels, and other changes to make the chart both more informative and more attractive. Part of this change will involve using the **RColorBrewer** package to set colors for the boxplots.

```
# GROUPED BOXPLOTS WITH OPTIONS

require("RColorBrewer")

boxplot(painters$Expression ~ painters$School,

        col = brewer.pal(8, "Pastel2"),

        names = c("Renais.",

                  "Mannerist",

                  "Seicento",

                  "Venetian",

                  "Lombard",

                  "16th C.",

                  "17th C.",
```

```
                    "French"),
    boxwex = 0.5,   # Width of box as proportion of original.
    whisklty = 1,   # Whisker line type; 1 = solid line
    staplelty = 0,  # Staple (line at end) type; 0 = none.
    outpch = 16,    # Symbols for outliers; 16 = filled circle.
    outcol = brewer.pal(8, "Pastel2"),   # Color for outliers.
    main = "Expression Ratings of Painters by School
            from \"painters\" Data set in \"MASS\" Package",
    xlab = "Painter's School",
    ylab = "Expression Ratings")
```

Note that there is no + or other line break in **main** for the title; R observes the break in the code as a typographic instruction. The improved boxplots are shown in Figure 27.

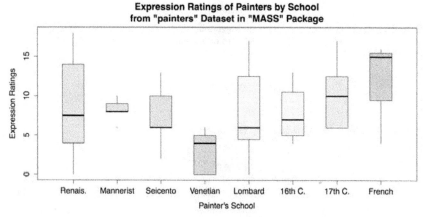

Figure 27: *Grouped Boxplots with Labels and Options*

Once you have saved your work, you should clean the workspace by removing any variables or objects you created.

```
# CLEAN UP
detach("package:MASS", unload = TRUE)  # Unloads MASS package
```

```
detach("package:RColorBrewer", unload = TRUE)  # Unloads RColorBrewer
package.
rm(list = ls())  # Remove all objects from workspace.
```

Scatter Plots

Perhaps the most common and most useful chart for visualizing the association between two variables is the scatter plot. Scatter plots are best used when the two variables are quantitative—that is, interval or ratio level of measurement—although they can be adapted to many other situations. In the base installation of R, the general-purpose **plot()** function is typically used for scatter plots. It works well both in its default configuration and with its many options. In addition, it is possible to overlay a variety of regression lines and smoothers.

For this example, we will use the **cars** data from R's **datasets** package.

Sample: sample_6_4.R

```
# LOAD DATA
require("datasets")  # Load datasets package.
data(cars)
```

Because the cars data set contains only two variables—**speed** and **dist** (i.e., distance to stop from the corresponding speed)—and both are quantitative, it is possible to have nothing more than the name of the data set as an argument to the **plot()** function.

```
# SCATTER PLOT WITH DEFAULTS
plot(cars)
```

This produces the scatter plot shown in Figure 28.

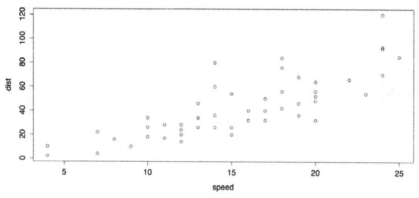

Figure 28:   *Default Scatter Plot with* `plot()`

And while the chart in Figure 28 is adequate, plot() also provides several options for labels and design.

```
# SCATTER PLOT WITH OPTIONS
plot(cars,
    pch = 16,
    col = "red",
    main = "Speed vs. Stopping Distance for Cars in
            1920s from \"cars\" Data set",
    xlab = "Speed (MPH)",
    ylab = "Stopping Distance (feet)")
```

The revised scatter plot is shown in Figure 29.

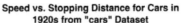

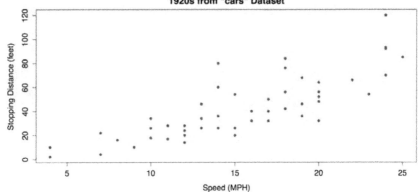

Figure 29: *Revised Scatter Plot with* plot()

The upward pattern that indicates a positive association between the two variables in Figure 29 is easy to see. However, the relationship can be even clearer if fit lines are added. In the following code, a linear regression line will be overlaid with the **abline()** function, which takes a linear regression model from the **lm()** function as its argument. In addition, a lowess line—locally weighted scatter plot smoothing—can be added with the **lines()** function, which takes the **lowess()** function as its argument. See **?abline**, **?lines**, and **?lowess** for more information on these functions.

```
# ADD REGRESSION & LOWESS
# Linear regression line.
abline(lm(cars$dist ~ cars$speed), col = "red")
# "locally weighted scatterplot smoothing"
lines(lowess(cars$speed, cars$dist), col = "blue")
```

The scatter plot with the added fit lines is shown in Figure 30.

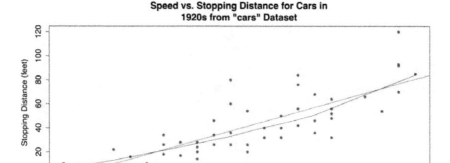

Figure 30: *Scatter Plot with Linear Regression and Lowess Fit Lines*

For a final variation on the bivariate scatter plot, we can use the **scatterplot()** or **sp()** function from the coincidentally named **car** package (which, in this case, stands for "Companion to Applied Regression"). This package has many variations on scatter plots. The one we will use has marginal boxplots, smoothers, and quantile regression intervals. See **help(package = "car")** for more information.

First we must install and load the **car** package.

```
# INSTALL & LOAD "CAR" PACKAGE
install.packages("car")  # Download the package.
require("car")  # Load the package.
```

Next, we can call the scatter plot function—which can be called with **scatterplot()** or **sp()**— with a few attribute arguments to alter the dots and provide titles and labels. Otherwise, the code is close to the default setup.

```
# "CAR" SCATTERPLOT
sp(cars$dist ~ cars$speed,  # Distance as a function of speed.
   pch = 16,  # Points: solid circles.
   col = "red",  # Red for graphic elements.
   main = "Speed vs. Stopping Distance for Cars in
           1920s from \"cars\" Data set",
   xlab = "Speed (MPH)",
   ylab = "Stopping Distance (feet)")
```

Figure 31 shows the resulting chart. The marginal boxplots, smoothers, and quantile regression intervals, all of which are included by default, make this a very information-dense graphic.

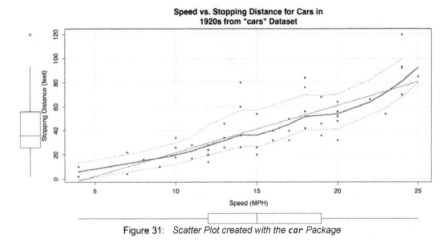

Figure 31: *Scatter Plot created with the car Package*

Once you have saved your work, clean the workspace by removing any variables or objects you created.

```
# CLEAN UP
detach("package:datasets", unload = TRUE)   # Unloads datasets package.
detach("package:car", unload = TRUE)   # Unloads car package.
rm(list = ls())   # Remove all objects from workspace.
```

Chapter 7 Statistics for Associations

In Chapter 6 we explored methods for visualizing the association between two variables. In this chapter, we will provide the complement to those analyses by discussing statistical procedures for describing bivariate associations. This chapter includes some of the most familiar inferential statistics: correlation, regression, t-tests for two samples and paired observations, the one-factor analysis of variance, tests to compare multiple proportions, and the chi-squared test for independence.

Correlations

Correlations are a mainstay of statistical analysis. R provides several approaches to correlations and the external packages provide an almost unlimited choice of procedures. In this section, we'll start with cor(), the default correlation function in R. We'll use the swiss data from R's datasets package. This data contains fertility and socio-economic variables for 47 French-speaking provinces of Switzerland in 1888. (See ?swiss for more information.)

Sample: sample_7_1.R

```
# LOAD DATA
require("datasets")   # Load the datasets package.
data(swiss)
```

Once the data are loaded into R, we can simply call the cor() function on the entire data frame. Also, to make the printout less busy, we can wrap the cor() function with the round() function to round the output to two decimal places.

```
# CORRELATION MATRIX
cor(swiss)
round(cor(swiss), 2)  # Rounded to 2 decimals
```

The first few rows and columns of that output are:

	Fertility	Agriculture	Examination	Education	Catholic
Fertility	1.00	0.35	-0.65	-0.66	0.46
Agriculture	0.35	1.00	-0.69	-0.64	0.40

Missing from this printout are probability values. R does not have a built-in function to get p-values—or even asterisks indicating statistical significance—for a correlation matrix. Instead, we can test each correlation separately with `cor.test()`. This function will give the correlation value, a hypothesis test, and a confidence interval for the correlation.

```
# INFERENTIAL TEST FOR SINGLE CORRELATION
cor.test(swiss$Fertility, swiss$Education)


        Pearson's product-moment correlation
data:  swiss$Fertility and swiss$Education
t = -5.9536, df = 45, p-value = 3.659e-07
alternative hypothesis: true correlation is not equal to 0
95 percent confidence interval:
 -0.7987075 -0.4653206
sample estimates:
       cor
-0.6637889
```

This is useful information but it is cumbersome to test correlations one at a time. The external package `Hmisc` provides an alternative, making it possible to get two matrices at once: one matrix with correlation values, and a second matrix with two-tailed p-values. The first step is to install and load the `Hmisc` package.

```
# INSTALL AND LOAD "HMISC" PACKAGE
install.packages("Hmisc")
require("Hmisc")
```

When you load `Hmisc`, you will receive message that R is also loading several other packages—`grid`, `lattice`, `survival`, `splines`, and `Formula`—that `Hmisc` relies on. You may also receive a message that a few functions, such as `format.pval`, `round.POSIXt`, `trunc.POSIXt`, and `units`, were masked from `package:base`. This happens because `Hmisc` is temporarily overriding those functions, which is supposed to happen, so you can ignore those messages.

Before we can run the `rcorr()` function from `Hmisc`, however, we need to make a change to our data. The `swiss` data are a data frame but `Hmisc` operates on matrices. All that we need to do is wrap `swiss` with the `as.matrix()` function, which can then be nested within `rcorr()`.

```
# COERCE DATA FRAME TO MATRIX
# GET R & P MATRICES
```

```
rcorr(as.matrix(swiss))
```

Here are the first few rows and columns of each resulting matrix. The first matrix consists of correlation coefficients and is identical to our rounded matrix from R's **cor()** function.

```
           Fertility Agriculture Examination Education Catholic

Fertility       1.00        0.35       -0.65     -0.66     0.46

Agriculture     0.35        1.00       -0.69     -0.64     0.40
```

The second matrix consists of two-tailed probability values, with blanks on the diagonal:

```
P
           Fertility Agriculture Examination Education Catholic
Fertility                 0.0149      0.0000    0.0000   0.0010
Agriculture     0.0149                0.0000    0.0000   0.0052
```

Using the standard criterion of $p < .05$, all of these correlations are statistically significant.

For more information on **Hmisc**, enter **help(package = "Hmisc")**. And, as before, when we are finished, we should unload the external packages and clear out any variables or objects we created.

```
# CLEAN UP
detach("package:datasets", unload=TRUE)  # Unload the package.
detach("package:Hmisc", unload=TRUE)  # Unload the package.
rm(list = ls())  # Remove the objects.
```

Bivariate regression

Bivariate regression—that is, linear regression between two variables—is a very common, flexible, and powerful procedure. R has excellent built-in functions for bivariate regression that can provide an enormous amount of information.

For this example, we will use the **trees** data from R's **datasets** package. (See **?trees** for more information.)

Sample: sample_7_2.R

```
# LOAD DATA
```

```
require("datasets")  # Load the datasets package.
data(trees)  # Load data into the workspace.
trees[1:5, ]  # Show the first 5 lines.
  Girth Height Volume
1   8.3     70   10.3
2   8.6     65   10.3
3   8.8     63   10.2
4  10.5     72   16.4
5  10.7     81   18.8
```

We will use bivariate regression to see how a tree's girth can predict its height. But first, it is always a good idea to check the variables graphically to see how well they meet the assumptions of our intended procedure.

```
# GRAPHICAL CHECK
hist(trees$Height)
hist(trees$Girth)
plot(trees$Girth, trees$Height)
```

To save space, I won't print those graphs here but I will mention that both variables are approximately normally distributed, with some positive skew on girth, and the scatter plot appears to be approximately linear. The variables appear well suited for regression analysis.

The command for linear regression is **lm()**. It requires only two arguments: the outcome variable and the predictor variable, with the tilde operator, ~, between them. For this example, it appears as **lm(Height ~ Girth, data = trees)**. The third argument here, **data = trees**, is optional. It is there to specify the data set from which the variables are drawn. As a note, it is also possible to give the full address for each variable, like **trees$Height** and **trees$Girth**. The separate **data** statement is just a convenience.

In this example, I am saving the regression model into reg1. By saving the model into an object, I am then able to call several functions on the model without having to specify it again. In the code that follows, I first run lm() and then get information on the model with **summary()**.

```
# BASIC REGRESSION MODEL
reg1 <- lm(Height ~ Girth, data = trees)  # Save the model.
summary(reg1)  # Get regression output.
Call:
lm(formula = Height ~ Girth, data = trees)
```

```
Residuals:
    Min      1Q   Median      3Q      Max
-12.5816  -2.7686   0.3163   2.4728   9.9456


Coefficients:
            Estimate Std. Error t value Pr(>|t|)
(Intercept)  62.0313     4.3833  14.152 1.49e-14 ***
Girth         1.0544     0.3222   3.272  0.00276 **
---
Signif. codes:  0 '***' 0.001 '**' 0.01 '*' 0.05 '.' 0.1 ' ' 1


Residual standard error: 5.538 on 29 degrees of freedom
Multiple R-squared:  0.2697,   Adjusted R-squared:  0.2445
F-statistic: 10.71 on 1 and 29 DF,  p-value: 0.002758
```

The **summary()** function gives nearly everything that is needed for most analyses: the regression coefficients, their statistical significance, the R^2 and adjusted R^2, the *F*-value and *p*-value for the entire model, and information about residuals. (See **?lm** and **?summary** for more information.)

It is also possible to get confidence intervals for the regression coefficients with the **confint()** function:

```
# CONFIDENCE INTERVALS
confint(reg1)
                2.5 %     97.5 %
(Intercept) 53.0664541 70.996174
Girth        0.3953483  1.713389
```

Other functions that can be useful when evaluating a regression model are:

- **predict()**, which gives the predicted values on the outcome variable for different value on the predictor (see **?predict**).
- **lm.influence()**, which gives basic quantities used in forming a wide variety of diagnostics for checking the quality of regression fits (see **?lm.influence**).
- **influence.measures()**, which gives information on residuals, dispersion, hat values, and others (see **?influence.measures**).

We can finish by unloading packages and cleaning the workspace:

```
# CLEAN UP
detach("package:datasets", unload = TRUE)  # Unloads data sets package.
rm(list = ls())  # Remove all objects from workspace.
```

Two-sample t-test

If you wish to compare the means of two different groups, then the most common choice is the two-sample t-test. R provides several options for this test and several ways to organize the data for analysis. For this example we will use the **sleep** data from R's **datasets** package. This data set, which was gathered by the creator of the t-test, William Gosset, who published under the pseudonym Student, shows the effect of two soporific drugs on 10 patients. The data set has three columns: **extra**, which is the increase in hours of sleep; **group**, which indicates the drug given; and **ID**, which is the patient ID. To make the analysis simpler, we will open the data, remove the ID variable, and save it as a new data frame called **sd** for "sleep data."

Sample: sample_7_3.R

```
# LOAD DATA & SELECT VARIABLES
require("datasets")  # Load the datasets package.
sleep[1:5, ]  # Show the first 5 cases.
sd <- sleep[, 1:2]  # Save just the first two variables.
sd[1:5, ]  # Show the first 5 cases.
```

Once the data are loaded into the new data frame, we can create some basic graphs, a histogram and a boxplot, to check on the shape of the distribution and how well it meets the statistical assumptions of the t-test.

```
# GRAPHICAL CHECKS
hist(sd$extra)  # Histogram of extra sleep.
boxplot(extra ~ group, data = sd)  # Boxplots by group.
```

To save space I will not reprint the graphics here, but I will say that the histogram is approximately normal and the boxplots, which are separated by group, do not show any outliers. With this preliminary check done, we can move ahead to the default t-test, using R's **t.test()** function.

```
# TWO-SAMPLE T-TEST WITH DEFAULTS
t.test(extra ~ group, data = sd)
        Welch Two Sample t-test
```

```
data:  extra by group
t = -1.8608, df = 17.776, p-value = 0.07939
alternative hypothesis: true difference in means is not equal to 0
95 percent confidence interval:
 -3.3654832  0.2054832
sample estimates:
mean in group 1 mean in group 2
          0.75            2.33
```

These results show that while there is a difference between the two group's means—2.33 vs. 0.75—the difference does not meet the conventional levels of statistical significance, as the observed p-value of .08 is greater than the standard cut-off of .05. As a note, R uses the Welch two-sample t-test by default, which is often used for samples with unequal variances. One consequence of this choice is that the degree of freedom is a fractional value, 17.776 in this case. For the more common, equal-variance t-test, just add the argument **var.equal = TRUE** to the function call (see **?t.test** for more information).

R's **t.test()** function also provides a number of options, such as one-tailed tests and different confidence levels, as show in the following code.

```
# TWO-SAMPLE T-TEST WITH OPTIONS
t.test(extra ~ group,  # Same: Specifies variables.
       data = sd,  # Same: Specifies data set.
       alternative = "less",  # One-tailed test.
       conf.level = 0.80)  # 80% CI (vs. 95%)


        Welch Two Sample t-test
data:  extra by group
t = -1.8608, df = 17.776, p-value = 0.0397
alternative hypothesis: true difference in means is less than 0
80 percent confidence interval:
        -Inf -0.8478191
sample estimates:
mean in group 1 mean in group 2
          0.75            2.33
```

As expected, when a one-tailed or directional hypothesis test is applied to the same data, the results are statistically significant with a p-value of .04 (exactly half of the p-value for the two-tailed test).

In the previous examples with the sleep data, the outcome variable was in one column and the grouping variable was in a second column. It is, however, also possible to have the data for each group in separate columns. In the following example, we will create simulated data using R's **rnorm()** function, which draws data from a normal distribution. One advantage of using simulated data is that it is possible to specify the differences between the groups exactly. It is also important to note that the data in this example will be slightly different every time the code is run, so your results should not match these exactly.

In this case, where the data for the two groups are in difference variables, the function call is simpler: just give the names of the two variables as the arguments to **t.test()**, as shown in the following code.

```
# SIMULATED DATA IN TWO VARIABLES
x <- rnorm(30, mean = 20, sd = 5)
y <- rnorm(30, mean = 24, sd = 6)
t.test(x, y)


        Welch's Two Sample t-test
data:  x and y
t = -2.6208, df = 56.601, p-value = 0.01124
alternative hypothesis: true difference in means is not equal to 0
95 percent confidence interval:
 -6.8721567 -0.9186296
sample estimates:
mean of x mean of y
 20.18359  24.07898
```

The results in this case indicate a statistically significant difference with a p-value of .01. Finally, we should tidy up by removing the packages and objects used in this section.

```
# CLEAN UP
detach("package:datasets", unload = TRUE)  # Unloads data sets package.
rm(list = ls())  # Remove all objects from workspace.
```

Paired t-test

The t-test is a flexible test with several variations. In the previous section we used the t-test to compare the means of two groups. In this section, we will use the t-test to examine how scores change over time for a single group of subjects. This is known as the paired t-test because each participant's observation at time 2 is paired with their own observation at time 1. The paired t-test is also known as the matched-subjects t-test or the within-subjects t-test.

In this example, we will use simulated data. In the code that follows, a variable called **t1**, for time 1, is created using the **rnorm()** function to generate normally distributed data with a specified mean and standard deviation (see **?rnorm** for more information). To simulate changes over time, another random variable, called **dif** for difference, is generated. These two variables are then summed to yield **t2**, the scores at time 2 for each subject.

Sample: sample_7_4.R

```
# CREATE SIMULATED DATA
t1 <- rnorm(50, mean = 52, sd = 6)  # Time 1
dif <- rnorm(50, mean = 6, sd = 12)  # Difference
t2 <- t1 + dif  # Time 2
```

Once the data are generated, the **t.test()** function can be called. The arguments in this case are the variables with the data at the two times, as well as **paired** = **TRUE**, which indicates that the paired t-test should be used.

```
# PAIRED T-TEST WITH DEFAULTS
t.test(t2, t1, paired = TRUE)  # Must specify "paired"


        Paired t-test
data:  t2 and t1
t = 4.457, df = 49, p-value = 4.836e-05
alternative hypothesis: true difference in means is not equal to 0
95 percent confidence interval:
  4.078233 10.775529
sample estimates:
mean of the differences
           7.426881
```

In this example, the change in scores over time was statistically significant. Note that your own results will be different because the data are generated at random. This effect can be seen in the following code, were the t-test is run again with several options: a non-zero null value is specified, a one-tailed test is called, and a different confidence level is used. The mean difference is smaller in this example (5.81 vs. 7.43) because the data were generated again before running this code.

```
# PAIRED T-TEST WITH OPTIONS
t.test(t2, t1,
       paired = TRUE,
       mu = 6,  # Specify a non-0 null value.
       alternative = "greater",  # One-tailed test
       conf.level = 0.99)  # 99% CI (vs. 95%)


        Paired t-test
data:  t2 and t1
t = -0.1027, df = 49, p-value = 0.5407
alternative hypothesis: true difference in means is greater than 6
99 percent confidence interval:
 1.529402     Inf
sample estimates:
mean of the differences
           5.816891
```

In this case the difference was not statistically significant, but that is due primarily to different null value used—6 vs. 0—and not to the variations in the datat.

We can finish by clearing the workspace.

```
# CLEAN UP
rm(list = ls())  # Remove all objects from the workspace.
```

One-factor ANOVA

The one-factor analysis of variance, or ANOVA, is used to compare the means of several different groups on a single, quantitative outcome variable. In this example we will again use simulated data from R's **rnorm()** function. As before, this means that your data will be slightly different, but the overall pattern should be the same. After the four variables are created with one variable for each group, they are combined into a single data frame using the **data.frame()** and **cbind()** functions. After that, the data need to be reorganized. The four separate variables are then stacked into a single outcome variable called **values** with the **stack()** function, which also creates a column called **ind** to indicate their source variable; this variable functions as the grouping variable.

Sample: sample_7_5.R

```
# CREATE SIMULATION DATA

# Step 1: Each group in a separate variable.

x1 <- rnorm(30, mean = 40, sd = 8)  # Group 1, mean = 40

x2 <- rnorm(30, mean = 41, sd = 8)  # Group 1, mean = 41

x3 <- rnorm(30, mean = 44, sd = 8)  # Group 1, mean = 44

x4 <- rnorm(30, mean = 45, sd = 8)  # Group 1, mean = 45


# Step 2: Combine vectors into a single data frame.

xdf <- data.frame(cbind(x1, x2, x3, x4))  # xdf = "x data frame"


# Step 3: Stack data to get the outcome column and group column.

xs <- stack(xdf)  # xs = "x stack"
```

At this point, the data are ready to be analyzed with R's **aov()** function. The default specification is simple, with just two required arguments: the outcome variable, which is **values** in this case, and the grouping variable, which is **ind** in this case. The two variables are joined by the tilde operator, ~. (The argument **data = xs** simply indicates the data frame that holds the variables.)

```
# ONE-FACTOR ANOVA
anova1 <- aov(values ~ ind, data = xs)  # Basic model.
summary(anova1)  # Model summary.
```

```
          Df Sum Sq Mean Sq F value Pr(>F)
ind        3    579  192.97   3.188 0.0264 *
Residuals 116   7022   60.53
---
Signif. codes:  0 '***' 0.001 '**' 0.01 '*' 0.05 '.' 0.1 ' ' 1
```

These results indicate that the omnibus analysis of variance is statistically significant, with a p-value of .03. However, this test does not indicate where the group differences lie. To find them, we need a post-hoc comparison. The default post-hoc procedure in R is Tukey's Honestly Significant Difference (HSD) test or `TukeyHSD()`.[19] Because we saved the ANOVA model into an object named anova1, we can just use that object as the argument in the code that follows:

```
# POST-HOC COMPARISONS
TukeyHSD(anova1)

  Tukey multiple comparisons of means
    95% family-wise confidence level
Fit: aov(formula = values ~ ind, data = xs)

$ind
            diff        lwr        upr      p adj
x2-x1  1.132450 -4.1039279  6.368829 0.9425906
x3-x1  5.502549  0.2661705 10.738927 0.0354399
x4-x1  4.004412 -1.2319658  9.240791 0.1964255
x3-x2  4.370098 -0.8662799  9.606477 0.1362299
x4-x2  2.871962 -2.3644162  8.108340 0.4835521
x4-x3 -1.498136 -6.7345146  3.738242 0.8782931
```

---

[19] See `?TukeyHSD` for more information on this procedure in particular. See `?pairwise.t.test` and `?p.adjust` for more information on post-hoc tests in R and specific procedures available.

The TukeyHSD() function reports observed differences between paired groups, as well as the lower and upper bounds for confidence intervals and adjusted p-values. What's interesting in this particular situation is that the only statistically significant difference is between groups 1 and 3. This is surprising because the commands that generated the random data actually called for a larger difference between groups 1 and 4. However, given the vicissitudes of random data generation, such quirks are to be expected. This is also an indication that sample size of 30 scores per group is probably not sufficiently large enough to give stable results.[20] In future research, it would be beneficial to at least double the sample size.

We can finish by cleaning the workspace of the variables and objects we generated in this exercise.

```
# CLEAN UP
rm(list = ls())   # Remove all objects from workspace
```

Comparing proportions

In the last five procedures that we examined—correlations, regression, two-sample t-tests, paired t-tests, and ANOVA—the outcome variable was quantitative (i.e., an interval or ratio level of measurement). This made it possible to calculate means and standard deviations, which were then used in the inferential tests. However, there are situations where the outcome variable is categorical (i.e., a nominal or possibly ordinal level of measurement.) The last two sections in this chapter address those situations. In the case of a dichotomous outcome—that is, an outcome with only two possible values, such as yes or no, on or off, and click or don't click, then a proportion test can be an ideal way to compare the performance of two or more groups.

In this example, we will again use simulated data. R's prop.test() function needs two pieces of information for each group: the number of trials or total observations, usually referred to as n, and the number of trials with positive outcome, usually referred to as X. In the code that follows, I create a vector called n5 of five 100s for the number of trials by using R's rep() function (see ?rep for more information). A second vector called x5 is then created with the number of positive outcomes for each group.

Sample: sample_7_6.R

```
# CREATE SIMULATION DATA
# Two vectors are needed:
# One specifies the total number of people in each group.
# This creates a vector with 5 100s in it, for 5 groups.
```

---

[20] Out of curiosity, I generated new data and ran the process a few more times. The second time, group 2 was different from groups 3 and 4 but that was all. The third time, group 4 was different from 1 and 2 and that was all. Again, the lesson is that larger samples are required for more stable estimates.

```
n5 <- c(rep(100, 5))
# Another specifies the number of cases with positive outcomes.
x5 <- c(65, 60, 60, 50, 45)
```

The next step is to call R's **prop.test()** function with two arguments: the variable with the X data and the variable with the n data.

```
# PROPORTION TEST
prop.test(x5, n5)

        5-sample test for equality of proportions without continuity
        correction

data:  x5 out of n5
X-squared = 10.9578, df = 4, p-value = 0.02704
alternative hypothesis: two.sided
sample estimates:
prop 1 prop 2 prop 3 prop 4 prop 5
  0.65   0.60   0.60   0.50   0.45
```

The output includes a chi-squared test—shown here as X-squared—and the p-value, which in this case is below the standard cutoff of .05. It also gives the observed sample proportions.

In the case where there are only two groups being compared, R will also give a confidence interval for the difference between the groups' proportions. The default value is .95 but that can be changed with the **conf.level** argument.

```
# CREATE SIMULATION DATA FOR 2 GROUPS
n2 <- c(40, 40)  # 40 trials
x2 <- c(30, 20)  # Number of positive outcomes
# PROPORTION TEST FOR 2 GROUPS
prop.test(x2, n2, conf.level = .80)  # With CI

        2-sample test for equality of proportions with continuity
        correction
data:  x2 out of n2
X-squared = 4.32, df = 1, p-value = 0.03767
```

```
alternative hypothesis: two.sided
80 percent confidence interval:
 0.09097213 0.40902787
sample estimates:
prop 1 prop 2
  0.75   0.50
```

In this case, despite the relatively small samples, the difference between the sample proportions is statistically significant, as shown by both the p-value and the confidence interval.

We can finish by clearing the workspace.

```
# CLEAN UP
rm(list = ls())  # Remove all objects from the workspace.
```

Cross-tabulations

The final bivariate procedure that we will discuss is the chi-squared inferential test for cross-tabulated data. In this example we will use the **Titanic** data from R's **datasets** package. This data contains the survival data from the wreck of the Titanic, broken down by sex, age (child or adult), and class of passenger (1st, 2nd, 3rd, or crew). See **?Titanic** for more information. The data are in a tabular format that, when displayed, consists of four 4 x 2 tables, although it is also possible to display it as a "flat" contingency table with the **ftable()** function.

Sample: sample_7_7.R

```
# LOAD DATA
require("datasets")  # Load the datasets package.
Titanic              # Show complete data in tables.
ftable(Titanic)      # Display a "flat" contingency table.
                      Survived  No Yes

Class Sex    Age
1st   Male   Child            0   5
             Adult          118  57
      Female Child            0   1
             Adult            4 140
2nd   Male   Child            0  11
             Adult          154  14
```

	Female	Child	0	13
		Adult	13	80
3rd	Male	Child	35	13
		Adult	387	75
	Female	Child	17	14
		Adult	89	76
Crew	Male	Child	0	0
		Adult	670	192
	Female	Child	0	0
		Adult	3	20

While the tabular format is a convenient way of storing and displaying the data, we need to restructure the data for our analysis so there is one row per observation. We can do this using a string of nested commands that we saw in sample_1_1.R:

```
# RESTRUCTURE DATA
tdf <- as.data.frame(lapply(as.data.frame.table(Titanic),
        function(x)rep(x, as.data.frame.table(Titanic)$Freq)))[, -5]
tdf[1:5, ]  # Check the first five rows of data.
  Class  Sex  Age Survived
1   3rd Male Child       No
2   3rd Male Child       No
3   3rd Male Child       No
4   3rd Male Child       No
5   3rd Male Child       No
```

For this example, we will focus on just two of the four variables: **Class** and **Survived**. To do this, we will create a reduced data set by using the **table()** function and save it into a new object, **ttab** for Titanic Table.

```
# CREATE REDUCED TABLE
ttab <- table(tdf$Class, tdf$Survived)  # Select two variables.
ttab  # Show the new table.
      No Yes
  1st 122 203
  2nd 167 118
```

```
3rd   528 178
Crew 673 212
```

The raw frequencies are important, but it easier to understand the pattern by looking at the row percentages. We can get these by using the **prop.table()** function and requesting the first column. In the code the follows, I also wrap these commands in the **round()** function to reduce the output to two decimal places, then multiply by 100 to get percentages.

```
# PERCENTAGES
rowp <- round(prop.table(ttab, 1), 2) * 100 # row %
colp <- round(prop.table(ttab, 2), 2) * 100 # column %
totp <- round(prop.table(ttab), 2) * 100     # total %
rowp
        No Yes
  1st   38  62
  2nd   59  41
  3rd   75  25
  Crew 76  24
```

From these results it is clear that first-class passengers had a much higher survival rate at 62%, while third-class passengers and crew had a much lower rate at 25% and 24%, respectively. The chi-squared test for independence, or R's **chisq.test()** function, can then test these results against a null hypothesis:

```
# CHI-SQUARED TEST FOR INDEPENDENCE
tchi <- chisq.test(ttab)  # Compare two variables in ttab
tchi

        Pearson's Chi-squared test
data:  ttab
X-squared = 190.4011, df = 3, p-value < 2.2e-16
```

Not surprisingly, these group differences are highly significant, with a p-value that is nearly zero. In addition to this basic output, R is able to give several other detailed tables from the saved chi-squared object:

- **tchi$observed** gives the observed frequencies, which is the same as data in **ttab**.
- **tchi$expected** gives the expected frequencies from the null distribution.
- **tchi$residuals** give the Pearson's residuals.
- **tchi$stdres** gives the standardized residuals based on the residual cell variance.

Finally, we can unload the packages and clear the workspace before moving on.

```
# CLEAN UP
detach("package:datasets", unload = TRUE)  # Unloads the datasets package.
rm(list = ls())  # Remove all objects from the workspace.
```

Chapter 8 Charts for Three or More Variables

The methods that we covered in Chapters 6 and 7 provided an initial approach to exploring the associations between variables, but those methods were limited to two variables at a time. Outside of a basic laboratory experiment, however, there is often a need to look at several variables at once. The methods that we will discuss in this chapter will allow us to do just that; they will allow us to visualize the connections between three or more variables at a time. The following chapter, Chapter 9, will then present methods for describing those complex relationships statistically.

Before we begin, a note about terminology is in order. When an analysis addresses one variable at a time, it's called a univariate analysis. When an analysis addresses the associations between pairs of variables, it's called a bivariate analysis. It would make sense, then, that an analysis that addressed multiple variables would be called a multivariate analysis. However, the term "multivariate" is typically reserved for situations where you specifically have more than one outcome variable. Those kinds of statistics are much more complicated than what we are going to be doing, which is using more than one predictor variable with a single outcome variable. With this in mind, I will generally avoid the term "multivariate" for these procedures and instead discuss "multiple variables."

Clustered bar chart for means

Our first chart will be a bar chart of means when there is more than one predictor variable. In this situation, a clustered bar chart is often the best choice. It is important to point out that many programs, such as Excel, PowerPoint, and similar programs, may offer to do three-dimensional charts with the bars laid out in a grid. Though there are situations where this would be a reasonable solution, they are rare. Three-dimensional charts are nearly always harder to read accurately than flat charts. For this same reason, adding a false thickness to the bars should be avoided. It simply complicates the charts without adding any usable information. Consequently, a side-by-side chart is typically a better choice as is easier to focus on the data and interpret it accurately.

For this exercise, we will use the **warpbreaks** data from R's **datasets** package. This data set gives the number of breaks in yarn in a loom according to the kind of yarn used (recorded as A and B) and the level of tension in the loom (recorded as L, M, and H, for low, medium, and high).

The first step is to load the **datasets** package and the **warpbreaks** data.

Sample: sample_8_1.R

```
# LOAD DATA
require("datasets")  # Load datasets package
```

```
data(warpbreaks)  # Load data into workspace
```

It would be convenient if these data could work directly with R's **barplot()** function, like this: **barplot(breaks ~ wool*tension, data = warpbreaks)**. Unfortunately, that will give an error message saying "**'height' must be a vector or a matrix**," meaning that the variable containing the height for the bars—which should be the mean number of breaks in this example—must have a different format. We can get the data into the correct format by using a combination of the **list()** function, which identifies the type of wool and the level of tension as factors (i.e., categorical predictor variables), and **tapply()**, which applies a function—**FUN = mean**, in this case—to a ragged array, or an array that may contain empty cells. We can then save the restructured data into a new object called **wbdata** for "warpbreaks data."

```
# RESTRUCTURE DATA

wbdata <- tapply(warpbreaks$breaks,  # Outcome
                 list(warpbreaks$wool, warpbreaks$tension),  # Factors
                 FUN = mean)  # Summary function
```

We can then use **wbdata** to create the bar plot.

```
# CREATE BARPLOT

barplot(wbdata,  # Use a new summary table.
        beside = TRUE,  # Bars side-by-side vs. stacked
        col = c("steelblue3", "thistle3"),  # Colors
        main = "Mean Number of Warp Breaks\nby Tension and Wool",
        xlab = "Tension",
        ylab = "Mean Number of Breaks")
```

Then we can add a legend using the interactive locator(1) function, which lets us choose a location by clicking the mouse on the plot.

```
# ADD LEGEND

legend(locator(1),  # Use mouse to locate the legend.
       rownames(wbdata),  # Use matrix row names (A & B)
       fill = c("steelblue3", "thistle3"))  # Colors
```

The resulting chart is shown in Figure 32.

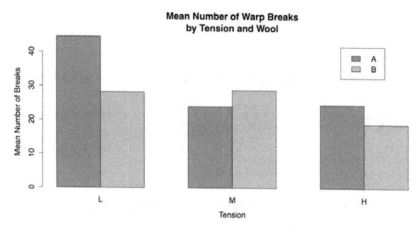

Figure 32: *Grouped Bar Plot for Means*

We can finish by cleaning up the workspace.

```
# CLEAN UP
detach("package:datasets", unload = TRUE)  # Unloads the datasets package.
rm(list = ls())  # Remove all objects from the workspace.
```

Scatter plots by groups

The clustered bar chart for means, which we looked at in the last section, is best used when you have two categorical predictor variables and a single quantitative outcome. If, instead, you have one categorical and one quantitative predictor for the quantitative outcome, then a grouped scatter plot can work well. This is simply a scatter plot in which the points are marked, usually by shape or color, according to the categorical variable. It is also possible to include separate fit lines such as linear regression lines or smoothers for each group.

For this example, we will use the `iris` data from R's **datasets** package.

Sample: sample_8_2.R

```
# LOAD DATA
require("datasets")  # Load the datasets package.
data(iris)  # Load data into workspace.
iris[1:3, ]  # Show the first three lines of data.
  Sepal.Length Sepal.Width Petal.Length Petal.Width Species
```

1	5.1	3.5	1.4	0.2	setosa
2	4.9	3.0	1.4	0.2	setosa
3	4.7	3.2	1.3	0.2	setosa

We will look at the relationship between sepal length and sepal width for the three different species in the iris data.

The easiest way to make a grouped scatter plot in R is with the external **car** package that we also used for the modified bivariate scatter plot in Chapter 6.

```
# LOAD "CAR" PACKAGE
require("car")  # "Companion to Applied Regression"
```

We will use the **scatterplot()** function, which can also be called with abbreviated name **sp()**. The important difference between this code and the command for the bivariate scatter plot is the addition of the pipe operator, |, which is used here to separate a grouping variable or factor— **Species**, in this case—from the rest of the function.

```
# SCATTERPLOT BY GROUPS
sp(Sepal.Width ~ Sepal.Length | Species,  # Group by species.
   data = iris,
   xlab = "Sepal Width",
   ylab = "Sepal Length",
   main = "Iris Data",
   labels = row.names(iris))  # Label names.
```

The resulting chart is shown in Figure 33.

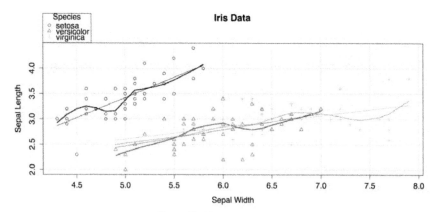

Figure 33: *Scatter Plot by Group*

The **car** package uses both colors and shapes to indicate group membership. By default, it also superimposes a linear regression line and a lowess smoother for each group, matched by color.

We can finish by unloading the packages and clearing the workspace.

```
# CLEAN UP
detach("package:datasets", unload = TRUE)  # Unloads the datasets package.
detach("package:car", unload = TRUE)  # Unloads the car package.
rm(list = ls())  # Remove all objects from workspace.
```

Scatter plot matrices

The grouped scatter plot we created in the last section was able to show the relationship between two quantitative variables while indicating group membership on a third, categorical variable. While that chart was impressively information-dense, it did not include all of the variables in the data set. To get all four quantitative variables in a chart, we need to do a scatter plot matrix, which is simply a collection of bivariate scatter plots. There are a few different ways to do this: R's default **pairs()** function, **pairs()** with a custom function, or the **scatterplotMatrix()** function from the **car** package. We will explore each approach, but first we need to load our data.

Sample: sample_8_3.R

```
require("datasets")  # Load the datasets package.
```

```
data(iris)  # Load data into the workspace.
iris[1:3, ]  # Show the first three lines of data.
  Sepal.Length Sepal.Width Petal.Length Petal.Width Species
1         5.1         3.5          1.4         0.2  setosa
2         4.9         3.0          1.4         0.2  setosa
3         4.7         3.2          1.3         0.2  setosa
```

The first approach we will use is R's **pairs()** function. The only argument needed for this function is the name a data frame. However, because the fifth variable in **iris** is categorical—the species name—we will exclude it by using only the first four columns of data.

```
# SCATTERPLOT MATRIX WITH DEFAULTS
pairs(iris[1:4])  # Use just the first four variables from iris.
```

The resulting plot is shown in Figure 34.

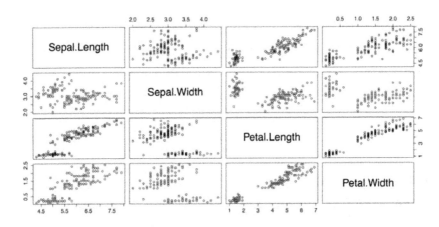

Figure 34: *Scatterplot Matrix with* **pairs()**

This is a reasonable plot, but it is not information-dense: there is no indication of group membership, there are no fit lines, and the large cells with the variable names could be used for other purposes.

We can fix these problems in a few steps. The first step is to augment the names on the diagonal with histograms for each variable. We can create a custom function for this with the following code, which was adapted from the code in **?pairs** in R's built-in help. It creates a new function called **panel.hist**. This function will be saved to the workspace and can then be called when we run the **pairs()** function again.

```
# FUNCTION TO PUT HISTOGRAMS ON DIAGONAL
# Adapted from code in "pairs" help
panel.hist <- function(x, ...)
{
  usr <- par("usr")  # Copies usr parameters for plot coordinates.
  on.exit(par(usr))  # Restores parameters on exit.
  par(usr = c(usr[1:2], 0, 1.5) )  # Sets plot coordinates.
  h <- hist(x, plot = FALSE)  # Creates histogram.
  breaks <- h$breaks  # Reads breaks for histograms.
  nB <- length(breaks)  # Reads number of breaks.
  y <- h$counts  # Get raw values for the y-axis.
  y <- y/max(y)  # Adjusts raw values to fit the y scale.
  rect(breaks[-nB], 0, breaks[-1], y,  ...)  # Draws boxes.
}
```

We can then load the **RColorBrewer** package so we can select a palette to indicate group membership in the plots.

```
# SET COLOR PALETTE WITH RCOLORBREWER
require("RColorBrewer")
```

After creating the **panel.hist** function and loading the **RColorBrewer** package, we can run the **pairs()** function again with several options specified. The **pairs()** function has a wide array of options, allowing us to choose, for example, which function will be displayed on the diagonal, the upper panel, the lower panel, etc. (See **?pairs** for more information.)

Also, the three species of iris are shown in different colors by calling the **RColorBrewer** palette **Pastel1** in the **col** attribute and using the **unclass()** function to break the **Species** factor into a list of ones, twos, and threes.

```
# SCATTERPLOT MATRIX WITH OPTIONS
pairs(iris[1:4],  # Reads the data.
      panel = panel.smooth,  # Adds an optional smoother.
```

```
      main = "Scatterplot Matrix for Iris Data Using pairs Function",
      diag.panel = panel.hist,  # Calls histogram function.
      pch = 16,  # Uses solid dots for points.
      # Next line color dots by "Species" category.
      col = brewer.pal(3, "Pastel1")[unclass(iris$Species)])
```

The resulting chart is shown in Figure 35.

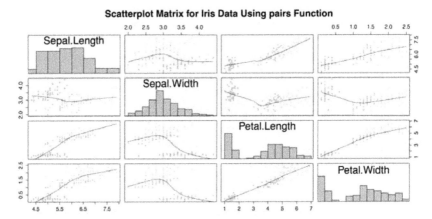

Figure 35: *Scatter Plot Matrix with Custom Function*

Figure 35 is an improvement over Figure 34, but it can still be improved. Most significantly, it is missing a legend to indicate group membership. It is also potentially troublesome to use a custom function with unknown compatibility issues. Instead, we can use the scatterplotMatrix() function from the car package. Also note in the code below the paste() function in the title attribute main. paste() puts separate strings together into a single string, which makes it possible to write a long title in the R command but keep the code from being too wide.

```
# SCATTERPLOT MATRIX WITH "CAR" PACKAGE
require("car")
scatterplotMatrix(~Petal.Length + Petal.Width +
                    Sepal.Length + Sepal.Width | Species,
                  data = iris,
                  main = paste("Scatterplot Matrix for Iris Data",
```

```
                              "Using the \"car\" Package"))
```

The previous command produces the chart shown in Figure 36.

Scatterplot Matrix for Iris Data Using the "car" Package

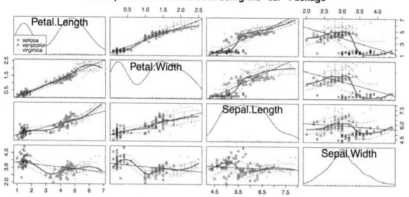

Figure 36: *Scatter Plot Matrix with the* `scatterplotMatrix()` *Function from the* **car** *Package*

Figure 36 accomplishes several things at once:

- It shows the relationship between four quantitative variables and one categorical variable.
- It marks group membership with colors and shapes.
- It provides a legend to the group variable.
- It provides a linear regression line for each plot.
- It provides a smoother with confidence intervals for each plot.
- It provides kernel density estimators with rugplots for each variable.

These factors make Figure 36 the most information-dense chart we have created in this book. This chart also serves as an example of the extraordinary flexibility and power of R, especially with the help of any of the thousands of external packages.

We can finish by returning the palette to the default, unloading the packages, and clearing our workspace.

```
# CLEAN UP

palette("default")  # Return to default.

detach("package:datasets", unload = TRUE)  # Unloads the datasets package.

detach("package:RColorBrewer", unload = TRUE)  # Unloads RColorBrewer

detach("package:car", unload=TRUE)  # Unloads car package.
```

```
rm(list = ls())   # Remove all objects from the workspace.
```

Chapter 9   Statistics for Three or More Variables

The final analytic chapter of this book addresses a few common methods for exploring and describing the relationships between multiple variables. These methods include the single most useful procedure in any analyst's toolbox, multiple regression. Other methods we will cover include the two-factor analysis of variance, the cluster analysis, and the principle components, or factor, analysis.

Multiple regression

The goal of regression is simple: take a collection of predictor variables and use them to predict scores on a single, quantitative outcome variable. Multiple regression is the most flexible approach we will cover in this book. All of the other parametric procedures that we have covered—t-tests, ANOVA, correlation, and bivariate regression—can all be seen as special cases of multiple regression.

In this section, we will start by looking at the simplest version of multiple regression: simultaneous entry. This is when all of the predictors are entered as a group and all of them are retained in the equation.

In this particular example, we're going to look at the most basic form of multiple regression, where all of the variables are entered at the same time in the equation (it's the variable selection and entry that causes most of the fuss in statistics). We will begin by loading the USJudgeRatings data from R's datasets package. See USJudgeRatings for more information.

Sample: sample_9_1.R

```
# LOAD DATA
require("datasets")  # Load the datasets package.
data(USJudgeRatings)  # Load data into the workspace.
USJudgeRatings[1:3, 1:8]  # Display 8 variables for 3 cases.
                CONT INTG DMNR DILG CFMG DECI PREP FAMI
AARONSON,L.H.   5.7  7.9  7.7  7.3  7.1  7.4  7.1  7.1
ALEXANDER,J.M.  6.8  8.9  8.8  8.5  7.8  8.1  8.0  8.0
ARMENTANO,A.J.  7.2  8.1  7.8  7.8  7.5  7.6  7.5  7.5
```

The default function in R for regression is **lm()**, which stands for "linear model" (see **?lm** for more information). The basic structure is **lm(outcome ~ predictor1 + predictor2)**. We can run this function on the outcome variable, **RTEN** (i.e., "worthy of retention"), and the eleven predictors using the code that follows and save the model to an object that we'll call **reg1**, for regression 1. Then, by calling only the name **reg1**, we can get the regression coefficients, and by calling **summary(reg1)**, we can get several statistics on the model.

```
# MULTIPLE REGRESSION: DEFAULTS
# Simultaneous entry
# Save regression model to the object.
reg1 <- lm(RTEN ~ CONT + INTG + DMNR + DILG + CFMG +
           DECI + PREP + FAMI + ORAL + WRIT + PHYS,
           data = USJudgeRatings)
```

Once we have saved the regression model, we can just call the object's name, **reg1**, and get a list of regression coefficients:

```
Coefficients:
(Intercept)        CONT        INTG        DMNR        DILG
   -2.11943     0.01280     0.36484     0.12540     0.06669
       CFMG        DECI        PREP        FAMI        ORAL
   -0.19453     0.27829    -0.00196    -0.13579     0.54782
       WRIT        PHYS
   -0.06806     0.26881
```

For more detailed information about the model, including descriptions of the residuals, confidence intervals for the coefficients, and inferential tests, we can just type **summary(reg1)**:

```
Residuals:
    Min      1Q  Median      3Q     Max
-0.22123 -0.06155 -0.01055 0.05045 0.26079


Coefficients:
            Estimate Std. Error t value Pr(>|t|)
(Intercept) -2.11943    0.51904  -4.083 0.000290 ***
CONT         0.01280    0.02586   0.495 0.624272
INTG         0.36484    0.12936   2.820 0.008291 **
```

```
DMNR        0.12540     0.08971    1.398 0.172102
DILG        0.06669     0.14303    0.466 0.644293
CFMG       -0.19453     0.14779   -1.316 0.197735
DECI        0.27829     0.13826    2.013 0.052883 .
PREP       -0.00196     0.24001   -0.008 0.993536
FAMI       -0.13579     0.26725   -0.508 0.614972
ORAL        0.54782     0.27725    1.976 0.057121 .
WRIT       -0.06806     0.31485   -0.216 0.830269
PHYS        0.26881     0.06213    4.326 0.000146 ***
---
Signif. codes:  0 '***' 0.001 '**' 0.01 '*' 0.05 '.' 0.1 ' ' 1

Residual standard error: 0.1174 on 31 degrees of freedom
Multiple R-squared:  0.9916,  Adjusted R-squared:  0.9886
F-statistic: 332.9 on 11 and 31 DF,  p-value: < 2.2e-16
```

All of the predictor variables are included in this model, which means that their coefficients and probability values are only valid when taken together. Two things are curious about this model. First, it has an extraordinarily high predictive value, with an R^2 of 99%. Second, the two most important predictors in this simultaneous entry model are (a) INTG, or judicial integrity, which makes obvious sense, and (b) PHYS, or physical ability, which has a t-value that's nearly twice as large as the integrity. This second one doesn't make sense but is supported by the data.

Additional information on the regression model is available with these functions, when the model's name is entered in the parentheses:

- anova(), which gives an ANOVA table for the regression model
- coef() or coefficients() which gives the same coefficients that we got by calling the model's name, reg1.
- confint(), which gives confidence intervals for the coefficients.
- resid() or residuals(), which gives case-by-case residual values.
- hist(residuals()), which gives a histogram of the residuals.

Multiple regression is potentially a very complicated procedure, with an enormous number of variations and much room for analytical judgment calls. The version that we conducted previously is the simplest version: all of the variables were entered at once in their original state (i.e. without any transformations), no interactions were specified, and no adjustments were made once the model was calculated.

R's base installation provides many other options and the available packages give hundreds, and possibly thousands, of other options for multiple regression.[21] I will just mention two of R's built-in options, both of which are based on stepwise procedures. Stepwise regression models work by using a simple criterion to include or exclude variables from a model, and they can greatly simplify analysis. Such models, however, are very susceptible to capitalizing on the quirks of data, leading one author, in exasperation, to call them "positively satanic in their temptations toward Type I errors."[22]

With those stern warnings in mind, we will nonetheless take a brief look at two versions of stepwise regression because they are very common—and commonly requested—procedures. The first variation we will examine is backwards removal, in which all possible variables are initially entered, and then variables that do make statistically significant contributions to the overall model are removed one at a time.

The first step is to create a full regression model, just like we did for simultaneous regression. Then, the R function **step()** is called with that regression model as its first argument and **direction = "backward"** as the second. An optional argument, **trace = 0**, prevents R from printing out all of the summary statistics at each step. Finally, we can use **summary()** to get summary statistics on the new model, which was saved as **regb**, as in "regression backwards."

```
# MULTIPLE REGRESSION: STEPWISE: BACKWARDS REMOVAL
reg1 <- lm(RTEN ~ CONT + INTG + DMNR + DILG + CFMG +
            DECI + PREP + FAMI + ORAL + WRIT + PHYS,
         data = USJudgeRatings)
regb <- step(reg1, # Stepwise regression, starts with the full model.
            direction = "backward", # Backwards removal
            trace = 0) # Don't print the steps.
summary(regb) # Give the hypothesis testing info.
Residuals:
     Min       1Q    Median        3Q       Max
-0.240656 -0.069026 -0.009474  0.068961  0.246402
```

---

[21] See the Regression Modeling Strategies package **rms** for one excellent example.

[22] That line is from page 185 of Norman Cliff's 1987 book, *Analyzing Multivariate Data*. Similar sentiments are expressed by Bruce Thompson in his 1998 talk "Five Methodology Errors in Educational Research: The Pantheon of Statistical Significance and Other Faux Pas," which lists stepwise methods as Error #1 (see http://people.cehd.tamu.edu/~bthompson/aeraaddr.htm), or his 1989 journal editorial entitled "Why won't stepwise methods die?" in *Measurement and Evaluation in Counseling and Development* (see http://myweb.brooklyn.liu.edu/cortiz/PDF%20Files/Why%20Wont%20Stepwise%20Methods%20Die.pdf). In simpler terms: analysts beware.

```
Coefficients:
              Estimate Std. Error t value Pr(>|t|)
(Intercept) -2.20433     0.43611  -5.055 1.19e-05 ***
INTG         0.37785     0.10559   3.579 0.000986 ***
DMNR         0.15199     0.06354   2.392 0.021957 *
DECI         0.16672     0.07702   2.165 0.036928 *
ORAL         0.29169     0.10191   2.862 0.006887 **
PHYS         0.28292     0.04678   6.048 5.40e-07 ***
---
Signif. codes:  0 '***' 0.001 '**' 0.01 '*' 0.05 '.' 0.1 ' ' 1

Residual standard error: 0.1119 on 37 degrees of freedom
Multiple R-squared:  0.9909,  Adjusted R-squared:  0.9897
F-statistic: 806.1 on 5 and 37 DF,  p-value: < 2.2e-16
```

Using a stepwise regression model with backwards removal, the predictive ability or R2 was still 99%. Only five variables remained in the model and, as with the simultaneous entry model, physical ability was still the single biggest contributor.

A more common approach to stepwise regression is forward selection, which starts with no variables and then adds them one at a time if they make statistically significant contributions to predictive ability. This approach is slightly more complicated in R because it requires the creation of a "minimal" model with nothing more than the intercept, which is the mean score on the outcome variable. This model is created by using the number 1 as the only predictor variable in the equation. Then the **step()** function is called again, with the minimal model as the starting point and **direction = "forward"** as one of the attributes. The possible variables to include are listed in **scope**. Finally, **trace = 0** prevents the intermediate steps from being printed.

```
# MULTIPLE REGRESSION: STEPWISE: FORWARDS SELECTION
# Start with a model that has nothing but a constant.
reg0 <- lm(RTEN ~ 1, data = USJudgeRatings)  # Intercept only
regf <- step(reg0,  # Start with intercept only.
          direction = "forward",  # Forward addition
          # scope is a list of possible variables to include.
          scope = (~ CONT + INTG + DMNR + DILG + CFMG + DECI +
                      PREP + FAMI + ORAL + WRIT + PHYS),
```

```
         data = USJudgeRatings,
         trace = 0)  # Don't print the steps.
summary(regf)  # Statistics on model.


Residuals:
    Min        1Q     Median        3Q       Max
-0.240656 -0.069026 -0.009474  0.068961  0.246402


Coefficients:
            Estimate Std. Error t value Pr(>|t|)
(Intercept) -2.20433    0.43611  -5.055 1.19e-05 ***
ORAL         0.29169    0.10191   2.862 0.006887 **
DMNR         0.15199    0.06354   2.392 0.021957 *
PHYS         0.28292    0.04678   6.048 5.40e-07 ***
INTG         0.37785    0.10559   3.579 0.000986 ***
DECI         0.16672    0.07702   2.165 0.036928 *
---
Signif. codes:  0 '***' 0.001 '**' 0.01 '*' 0.05 '.' 0.1 ' ' 1

Residual standard error: 0.1119 on 37 degrees of freedom
Multiple R-squared:  0.9909,   Adjusted R-squared:  0.9897
F-statistic: 806.1 on 5 and 37 DF,  p-value: < 2.2e-16
```

Given the possible fluctuations of stepwise regression, it is reassuring to know that both approaches finished with the same model, although they are listed in a different order.

Again, it is important to remember that multiple regression can be a very complicated and subtle procedure and that many analysts have criticized stepwise methods vigorously. Fortunately, R and its available packages offer many alternatives—and more are added on a regular basis—so I would encourage you to explore you options before committing to a single approach.

Once you have saved your work, you should clean the workspace by removing any variables or objects you created.

```
# CLEAN UP
detach("package:datasets", unload = TRUE)  # Unloads the datasets package.
rm(list = ls())  # Remove all objects from the workspace.
```

Two-factor ANOVA

The multiple regression procedure that we discussed in the previous section is enormously flexible, and the procedure that we will discuss in this section, the two-factor analysis of variance (ANOVA), can accurately be described as a special case of multiple regression. There are, however, advantages to using the specialized procedures of ANOVA. The most important advantage is that it was developed specifically to work in situations where two categorical variables—called *factors* in ANOVA—are used simultaneously to predict a single quantitative outcome. ANOVA gives easily interpreted results for the main effect of each factor and a third result for their interaction. We will examine these effects by using the **warpbreaks** data from R's **datasets** package.

Sample: sample_9_2.R

```
# LOAD DATA
require("datasets")  # Load the datasets package.
data(warpbreaks)
```

There are two different ways to specify a two-factor ANOVA in R, but both use the **aov()** function. In the first method, the main effects and interaction are explicitly specified, as shown in the following code. The results of that analysis can be viewed with the **summary()** function that we have used elsewhere.

```
# ANOVA: METHOD 1
aov1 <- aov(breaks ~ wool + tension + wool:tension,
            data = warpbreaks)
summary(aov1)  # ANOVA table
              Df Sum Sq Mean Sq F value   Pr(>F)
wool           1    451   450.7   3.765 0.058213 .
tension        2   2034  1017.1   8.498 0.000693 ***
wool:tension   2   1003   501.4   4.189 0.021044 *
Residuals     48   5745   119.7
---
Signif. codes:  0 '***' 0.001 '**' 0.01 '*' 0.05 '.' 0.1 ' ' 1
```

These results show a strong main effect of level of tension on the breakage of wool, with a smaller interaction with the kind of wool used. These results make sense, given the pattern of means we saw in the grouped bar chart back in Chapter 8. Figure 32 is reproduced below as Figure 37 for your convenience:

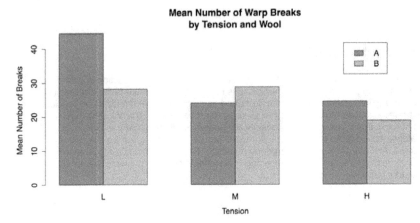

Figure 37: *Grouped Bar Chart of Mean*

A second method for specifying the ANOVA spells out only the interaction and leaves the main effects as implicit, with the same results as the first method.

```
# ANOVA: METHOD 2
aov2 <- aov(breaks ~ wool*tension,
            data = warpbreaks)
```

R is also able to provide a substantial amount of additional information via the **model.tables()** function. For example, the command **model.tables(aov1, type = "means")** gives tables of all the marginal and cell means, while the command **model.tables(aov1, type = "effects")** reinterprets those means as coefficients.

Finally, if one or both of the factors has more than two levels, it may be necessary to do a post-hoc test. As with the one-factor ANOVA discussed in Chapter 7, a good choice is Tukey's HSD (Honestly Significant Difference) test, with the R command **TukeyHSD()**.

We can finish this section by unloading and packages and clearing the workspace.

```
# CLEAN UP
detach("package:datasets", unload = TRUE)   # Unloads the datasets package.
rm(list = ls())   # Remove all objects from workspace.
```

Cluster analysis

Cluster analysis performs a fundamental task: determining which cases are similar. This task makes it possible to place cases—be they people, companies, regions of the country, etc.—into relatively homogeneous groups while distinguishing them from other groups. R has built-in functions that approach the formation of clusters in two ways. The first approach is k-means clustering with the kmeans() function. This approach requires that the researcher specify how many clusters they would like to form, although it is possible to try several variations. The second approach is hierarchical clustering with the hclust() function, in which each case starts by itself and then the cases are gradually joined together according to their similarity. We will discuss these two procedures in turn.

For these examples we will use a slightly reduced version of the mtcars data from R's datasets package, where we remove two undefined variables from the data set.

Sample: sample_9_3.R

```
# LOAD DATA
require("datasets")  # Load the datasets package.
mtcars1 <- mtcars[, c(1:4, 6:7, 9:11)]  # New object, select variables.
mtcars1[1:3, ]  # Show the first three lines of the new object.
              mpg cyl disp  hp   wt  qsec am gear carb
Mazda RX4      21.0  6  160 110 2.620 16.46  1    4    4
Mazda RX4 Wag  21.0  6  160 110 2.875 17.02  1    4    4
Datsun 710     22.8  4  108  93 2.320 18.61  1    4    1
```

In order to use the kmeans() function, we must specify the number of clusters we want. For this example, we'll try three clusters, although further inspection might suggest fewer or more clusters. This function produces a substantial amount of output that can be displayed by calling the name of the object with the results, which would be km in this case.

```
# CLUSTER ANALYSIS: K-MEANS
km <- kmeans(mtcars1, 3)  # Specify 3 clusters
```

Instead of the statistical output for the kmeans() function, it is more useful at this point to create a graph of the clusters. Unfortunately, the kmeans() function does not do this by default. We will instead use the clusplot() function from the cluster package.

```
# USE "CLUSTER" PACKAGE FOR K-MEANS GRAPH
require("cluster")
clusplot(mtcars1,       # Data frame
         km$cluster,    # Cluster data
```

```
    color = TRUE,     # Use color
    shade = FALSE,    # Colored lines in clusters (FALSE is default).
    lines = 3,        # Turns off lines connecting centroids.
    labels = 2)       # Labels clusters and cases.
```

This command produces the chart shown in Figure 38.

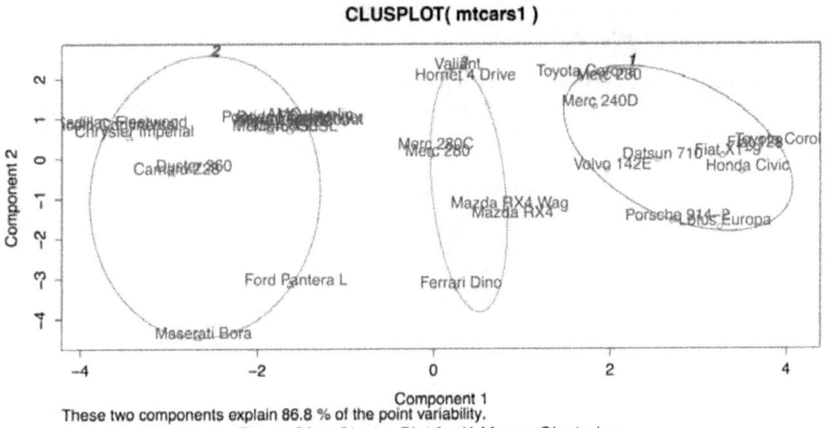

Figure 38: *Cluster Plot for K-Means Clustering*

Figure 38 shows the three clusters bound by colored circles and arranged on a grid defined by the two largest cluster components. There is good separation between the clusters, but the large separation in cluster 2 on the far left suggests that more than three clusters might be appropriate. Hierarchical clustering would be a good method for checking on the number and size of clusters.

In R, hierarchical clustering is done with the hclust() function. However, this function does not run on the raw data frame. Instead, it needs a distance or dissimilarity matrix, which can be created with the dist() function. Once the dist() and hclust() functions are run, it is then possible to display a dendrogram of the clusters using R's generic plot() command on the model generated by hclust().

```
# HIERARCHICAL CLUSTERING
d <- dist(mtcars1)   # Calculate the distance matrix.
c <- hclust(d)   # Use distance matrix for clustering.
plot(c)   # Plot a dendrogram of clusters.
```

Figure 39 shows the default dendrogram produced by `plot()`. In this plot, each case is listed individually at the bottom. The lines above join each case to other similar cases, while cases that are more similar are joined lower down—such as the Mercedes-Benz 280 and 280C on the far right—and cases that are more different are joined higher up. For example, it is clear from this diagram that the Maserati Bora on the far left is substantially different from every other car in the data set.

Cluster Dendrogram

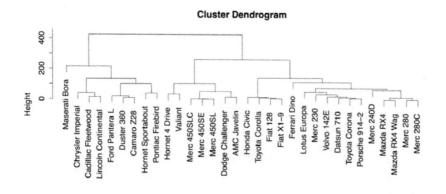

d
hclust (*, "complete")
Figure 39: *Hierarchical Clustering Dendrogram with Defaults*

Once the hierarchical model has been calculated, it is also possible to place the observations into groups using `cutree()`, which represents a "cut tree" diagram, another name for a dendrogram. You must, however, tell the function how or where to cut the tree into groups. You can specify either the number of groups using **k = 3**, or you can specify the vertical height on the dendrogram, **h = 230**, which would produce the same result. For example, the following command will categorize the cases into three groups and then show the group IDs for the last three cases:

```
# PLACE OBSERVATIONS IN GROUPS
g3 <- cutree(c, k = 3)  # "g3" = "groups: 3"
g3[30:32]  # Show groups for the last three cases.
Ferrari Dino Maserati Bora    Volvo 142E
           1            3             1
```

As a note, it is also possible to do several groupings at once by specifying a range of groups (**k = 2:5** will do groups of 2, 3, 4, and 5) or specific values (**k = c(2, 4)** will do groups of 2 and 4).

A final convenient feature of R's hierarchical clustering function is the ability to draw boxes around groups in the dendrogram using `rect.hclust()`. The following code superimposes four sets of different colored boxes on the dendrogram:

```
# DRAW BORDERS AROUND CLUSTERS
rect.hclust(c, k = 2, border = "gray")
rect.hclust(c, k = 3, border = "blue")
rect.hclust(c, k = 4, border = "green4")
rect.hclust(c, k = 5, border = "red")
```

The result is shown in Figure 40.

Cluster Dendrogram

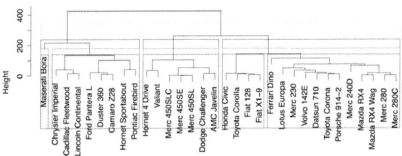

d
hclust (*, "complete")

Figure 40: *Hierarchical Clustering Dendrogram with Boxes around Groups*

From Figure 40, it is clear that large, American cars form groups that are distinct from smaller, imported cars. It is also clear, again, that the Maserati Bora is distinct from the group, as it is placed in its own category once we request at least four groups.

Once you have saved your work, you should clean the workspace by removing any variables or objects you created.

```
# CLEAN UP
detach("package:datasets", unload = TRUE)  # Unloads datasets package.
detach("package:cluster", unload = TRUE)  # Unloads datasets package.
rm(list = ls())  # Remove all objects from the workspace.
```

Principal components and factor analysis

The final pair of statistical procedures that we will discuss in this book is principal components analysis (PCA) and factor analysis (FA). These procedures are very closely related and are commonly used to explore relationships between variables with the intent of combining variables into groups. In that sense, these procedures are the complement of cluster analysis, which we covered in the last section. However, where cluster analysis groups cases, PCA and FA group variables. PCA and FA are terms that are often used interchangeably, even if that is not technically correct. One explanation of the differences between the two is given in the documentation for the psych package: "The primary empirical difference between a components model versus a factor model is the treatment of the variances for each item. Philosophically, components are weighted composites of observed variables while in the factor model, variables are weighted composites of the factors."[23] In my experience, that can be a distinction without a difference. I personally have a very pragmatic approach to PCA and FA: the ability to interpret and apply the results is the most important outcome. Therefore, it sometimes helps to see the results of these analyses more as recommendations on how the variables could be grouped rather than as statistical dogma that must be followed.

With that caveat in mind, we can look at a simple example of how to run PCA and then FA in R. For this example, we will use the same mtcars data from R's **datasets** package that we used in the last section to illustrate cluster analysis. We will exclude two variables from the data set because R does not provide explanations of their meaning. That leaves us with nine variables to work with.

Sample: sample_9_4.R

```
# LOAD DATA
require("datasets")  # Load the datasets package.
mtcars1 <- mtcars[, c(1:4, 6:7, 9:11)]  # Select the variables.
mtcars1[1:3, ]  # Show the first three cases.
                mpg cyl disp  hp    wt  qsec am gear carb
Mazda RX4      21.0   6  160 110 2.620 16.46  1    4    4
Mazda RX4 Wag  21.0   6  160 110 2.875 17.02  1    4    4
Datsun 710     22.8   4  108  93 2.320 18.61  1    4    1
```

The default method for principal components analysis in R is **prcomp()**. This function is easiest to use if the entire data frame can be used. Also, there are two additional arguments that can standardize the variables and make the results more interpretable: **center = TRUE**, which centers the variables' means to zero, and **scale = TRUE**, which sets their variance to one (i.e., unit variance). These two arguments essentially turn all of the observations into z-scores and ensure that the data have a form of homogeneity of variance, which helps stabilize the results of principal components analysis See **?prcomp** for more information on this function and the **center** and **scale** arguments.

---

[23] See page 230 of http://cran.r-project.org/web/packages/psych/psych.pdf.

```
# PRINCIPAL COMPONENTS
pc <- prcomp(mtcars1,
            center = TRUE,  # Centers means to 0 (optional).
            scale = TRUE)  # Sets unit variance (helpful).
```

By saving the analysis in an object—pc in this case—we can call additional functions for several functions. The first is **summary()**, which gives the proportion of total variance accounted for by each component. The first line, "standard deviation," contains the square roots of the eigenvalues of the covariance/correlation matrix.

```
# OUTPUT
summary(pc)  # Summary statistics
Importance of components:
                         PC1    PC2     PC3     PC4     PC5     PC6     PC7
Standard deviation     2.3391 1.5299 0.71836 0.46491 0.38903 0.35099 0.31714
Proportion of Variance 0.6079 0.2601 0.05734 0.02402 0.01682 0.01369 0.01118
Cumulative Proportion  0.6079 0.8680 0.92537 0.94939 0.96620 0.97989 0.99107
                         PC8    PC9
Standard deviation     0.24070 0.1499
Proportion of Variance 0.00644 0.0025
Cumulative Proportion  0.99750 1.0000
```

Some plots are also available for PCA. The generic **plot()** function, when applied to the output of **prcomp()**, will give an unlabeled bar chart of the eigenvalues for each component, although that can be used to give an intuitive test of how many components should be retained.

The function **biplot()** gives a two dimensional plot with:

1. The two largest components on the X and Y axes, respectively.
2. Vectors to indicate the relationship of each variable in the data frame to those components.
3. The labels for the individual cases to show where they fall on the two components.

With our data, **biplot(pc)** will give Figure 41.

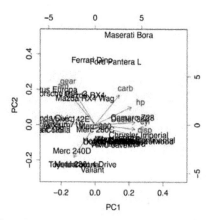

Figure 41: *Biplot of the Principal Components Analysis*

The simplest use of factor analysis (FA) within R is to determine how many factors are needed to adequately represent the variability within the data. For example, in our data, we can run several iterations of the function **factanal()**, where we specify different numbers of possible factors and check the probability values on the resulting chi-squared test. In this case, we are looking for a model that is *not* statistically significant (i.e., $p > .05$ as opposed to $p < .05$) because we want a model that corresponds well with the data and does not deviate substantially from it. In each of the following four analyses, a different number of factors is specified and the p-value from the last line of the printout is mentioned. The complete printout for the final command is also included.

```
# FACTOR ANALYSIS
factanal(mtcars1, 1)  # 1 factor, p < .05 (poor fit)
factanal(mtcars1, 2)  # 2 factors, p < .05 (poor fit)
factanal(mtcars1, 3)  # 3 factors, p < .05 (poor fit)
factanal(mtcars1, 4)  # 4 factors, First w/p > .05 (good fit)
Call:
factanal(x = mtcars1, factors = 4)


Uniquenesses:
  mpg   cyl  disp    hp    wt  qsec    am  gear  carb
0.137 0.045 0.005 0.108 0.038 0.101 0.189 0.126 0.031


Loadings:
```

```
        Factor1 Factor2 Factor3 Factor4
mpg    0.636  -0.445  -0.453  -0.234
cyl   -0.601   0.701   0.277   0.163
disp  -0.637   0.555   0.176   0.500
hp    -0.249   0.721   0.472   0.296
wt    -0.730   0.219   0.417   0.456
qsec  -0.182  -0.897  -0.246
am     0.891                  -0.100
gear   0.907           0.226
carb           0.478   0.851


                Factor1 Factor2 Factor3 Factor4
SS loadings      3.424   2.603   1.549   0.644
Proportion Var   0.380   0.289   0.172   0.072
Cumulative Var   0.380   0.670   0.842   0.913


Test of the hypothesis that 4 factors are sufficient.
The chi square statistic is 6.06 on 6 degrees of freedom.
The p-value is 0.416
```

These results suggest from the pattern of factor loadings that the first factor has to do with physical size of a car (with smaller cars getting higher factor scores), the second factor has to do with power and speed (with higher scores for more powerful and quicker cars), the third factor has to do with carburetor barrels (which reduces to the "Maserati Bora" factor, as it was the only car with eight carburetor barrels), and the fourth factor gives some additional variance to heavier cars with larger engines. These results can be compared with the biplot that came from the PCA and the cluster analysis in the previous section to provide a more complete understanding of the relationships between cases and variables in this data set.

Once you have saved your work, you should clean the workspace by removing any variables or objects you created.

```
# CLEAN UP
detach("package:datasets", unload = TRUE)  # Unloads the datasets package.
rm(list = ls())  # Remove all objects from the workspace.
```

Chapter 10 Conclusion

Next steps

This book has been, of necessity, a short one that was designed primarily to give you a flavor what R could do for you and how you could use it in your own work. The depth and breadth of R—especially when coupled with its contributed packages—make it impossible for any one book to do it justice. But hopefully this will serve as a jumping off point for some of your own explorations with R.

Before we go, I wanted to give you a short list of possible next steps for learning about statistical programming and data analysis. These resources include books and websites, associated software, and local and global events for users of R.

Books

The growing popularity of R is mirrored in the increasing collection of books that are available. Some excellent resources include:

- *An Introduction to R* by The R Core Team, available here.
- *The R Book* by Michael J. Crawley
- *Statistics: An Introduction Using R* by Michael J. Crawley
- *R in a Nutshell: A Desktop Quick Reference (2e)* by Joseph Adler
- *R Cookbook* by Paul Teetor
- *R Graphics Cookbook* by Winston Chang
- *ggplot2: Elegant Graphics for Data Analysis* by Hadley Wickham
- *Lattice: Multivariate Data Visualization* with R by Deepayan Sarkar
- *Learning RStudio for R Statistical Computing* by Mark van der Loo and Edwin de Jonge
- *Getting Started with RStudio* by John Verzani
- Many more are listed here.

Websites

In addition to published books, several online resources are of great value. Surprisingly, a conventional Google search with the letter R and the topic of interest will nearly always lead to sites related to this software. Here are a few resources I've found:

- The R Project website
- The R Journal is the open access, refereed journal of the R project for statistical computing.
- R-bloggers, news and tutorials about R, contributed by over 400 bloggers. There are 200-300 new posts each month.
- Rseek.org by Sasha Goodman
- Stack Overflow has great discussions on R.

- Wikibooks: R Programming Wikibook
- Quick-R
- ggplot2 website by Hadley Wickham

Software

For developers who are comfortable working with C++, Dirk Eddelbuettel and Romain Francois have developed **Rcpp**, an integration of R and C++ that can provide dramatic improvements in processing speed.

- Rcpp by Dirk Eddelbuettel and Romain Francois
  - Tutorial by Hadley Wickham

Events

International and local groups meet to present research using R and new methods that can be applied in your own research:

- useR! is an international conference that takes place in June or July of each year
  - The 2013 conference was at the University of Castilla-La Mancha in Albacete, Spain.
  - The 2014 conference was at UCLA in Los Angeles, California.
- Local R User Groups
  - See the full list at Revolution Analytics.

Conclusion

Hopefully this book has left you excited about the possibilities of using R, and motivated to learn more and even return the favor by contributing to the R community. Thanks for joining me. Good luck with your own explorations!

www.ingramcontent.com/pod-product-compliance
Lightning Source LLC
Chambersburg PA
CBHW071254050326
40690CB00011B/2390